P9-CRB-720

The Grolier Illustrated

Encyclopedia

of

Animals

Grolier Educational Corporation, 1994

This revised and updated library edition published by
Grolier Educational Corporation, 1994.
Copyright © Grisewood & Dempsey 1984, 1992.
All rights reserved under International and
Pan-American Copyright Conventions.

2 4 6 8 10 9 7 5 3

ISBN: 0-7172-7302-4 Cataloging information may be
obtained from the Grolier Educational Corporation,
Sherman Turnpike, Danbury, Connecticut 06816.
Printed in Italy.

THE GROLIER ILLUSTRATED
ENCYCLOPEDIA
OF
ANIMALS

From Aardvark to Zorille — and 2,000 other Animals

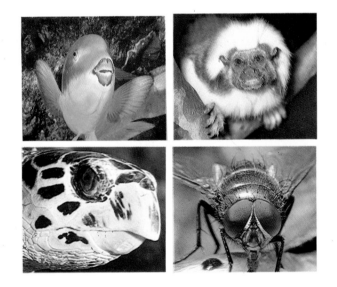

Consultant Editor: Michael Chinery

VOLUME 1

 Grolier Educational Corporation
DANBURY, CONNECTICUT

Explanation of Endangerment Status Code

This encyclopedia includes an update on the status of animals that are at risk of becoming endangered or extinct. A letter denoting the status of those animals or species at risk can be found opposite the entry heading. (If no letter appears, it means that no species of that animal is endangered.)

An extinct (Ex) animal is one that has not been found in the wild for 50 years, as is the case of the Tasmanian wolf. Animals in great danger of becoming extinct are considered endangered (E) species. One famous example is the giant panda. An animal such as the bactrian camel is labeled vulnerable (V), because it is likely to become endangered in the near future. Rare (R) animals, such as the hamadryas and gelada baboons, are at risk of becoming vulnerable or endangered.

For some animal families only a few species are endangered, while many species are not endangered (N). Some animals may have more than one letter opposite the entry heading. This indicates that the endangerment risk varies among the species of this animal, and more specific information about the population status of this animal may be described in the text. For example, the entry for mouse includes the letters N, R, V, E, Ex, indicating that while many mouse species are not endangered, some are rare, others are vulnerable or endangered, and some are extinct.

For further information about endangered species, see the Grolier World Encyclopedia of Endangered Species, or the 1990 IUCN Red List of Threatened Animals.

Extinct (Ex)—species not found in the wild for 50 years.
Endangered (E)—animals that are in great danger of becoming extinct.
Vulnerable (V)—species that are likely to become endangered in the near future.
Rare (R)—animals that are at risk of becoming vulnerable or endangered.
Not endangered (N)—some species are not endangered.

INTRODUCTION

More than a million kinds of animal have been discovered on the Earth so far, and many more will undoubtedly be discovered as people continue to explore the forests and seas and the many other habitats on our planet.

The animals form one of the two great kingdoms of the living world; the other is the plants. Because of the immense variety of animal life – ranging from minute protozoans visible only through a microscope to the huge blue whale, 100 feet (30 m) long and over 100 tons in weight – it is not easy to define an animal. But there are a number of features which, taken together, separate most animals from most plants.

The biggest difference is in the method of feeding, or obtaining energy. Unlike green plants, animals cannot make their own food, and they have to take in ready-made food in the form of other animal or plant matter. Such food has to be found, and most animals are therefore able to move around freely. They also have nervous systems to control their movements, and sense organs to help them to find suitable food.

Taken together, these features readily distinguish all the larger animals from the plants, but there are still a number of microscopic organisms that defy a firm classification. These include free-swimming creatures with sensitive eyespots, which sometimes feed like plants – by taking in water and carbon dioxide and combining them to form sugars – and sometimes take in food like animals. Zoologists claim these creatures as animals, botanists treat them as algae, while a few biologists actually put them into a separate kingdom known as the Protista. However we classify these "difficult" organisms, we can be fairly sure that it was through creatures like this that both the animal and plant kingdoms arose some two billion years ago.

Classifying Animals

Zoologists have divided the animal kingdom into about 30 major groups called *phyla*. The members of each phylum share the same basic structure and organization, although they may look very different. Fish, birds, and humans, for example, all belong to one phylum – the Chordata – because all have backbones, but their external appearances are totally different.

The phyla are divided up into a number of *classes*, whose members have much more in common. All the birds, for example, are warm-blooded, feathered, egg-laying creatures and all are placed in the class Aves.

Classes are divided into *orders*, and the members of an order have even more in common with each other. The Falconiformes, for example, contains the hawks and eagles and their relatives – all day-flying birds of prey with sharp talons and hooked beaks.

Within each order, there are usually a number of *families*, each of which contains very closely related kinds of animals. In the animal kingdom, a family name always ends in -idae.

Within each family, there are one or more *genera* (singular: genus), whose members are even more closely related and often very similar. For example, the buzzard and the rough-legged buzzard are much alike, and both are members of the genus *Buteo*. Each distinct kind, or species, of animal has a scientific name made up of the name of its genus and a specific name. For example, the rough-legged buzzard is known as *Buteo lagopus*, while the buzzard is *Buteo buteo*. These scientific names, which are usually printed in italics, are understood by zoologists all over the world.

The members of each animal species contain the "blueprint" for that species in the cells of their bodies and, because they usually mate only with their own kind, they automatically produce more of the same kind when they breed. Animals are not normally attracted to other species for mating because they don't give the right signals, and mating between different species is often physically impossible even if they meet. Closely related species do occasionally mate in captivity, however, and the offspring of such pairings are called hybrids. The best known example is the mule, resulting from the mating of a male ass or donkey and a female horse. Hybrids are generally sterile, however, and cannot produce further offspring, and so the species do not become mixed up.

With or Without Backbones
One commonly used method of splitting up the animal kingdom is to divide it into animals with backbones (vertebrates) and animals without backbones (invertebrates). This is quite a useful division, especially for study and teaching purposes, but it is a very unequal division. There are invertebrate animals in all the phyla, but the vertebrates belong to just one part of one phylum – the Chordata. The vertebrates include the largest animals and most of the familiar ones, such as cats, dogs, horses, cows, and birds. They also include all the fish, amphibians, and reptiles. The invertebrates include the worms, slugs, snails, insects, spiders, and many others. But it must not be thought that all the vertebrates are large and all the invertebrates small. The largest invertebrates – the giant squids of the genus *Architeuthis* – have bodies that are about 16 feet (5 m) long, with tentacles three times this length. They weigh up to two tons. Compare these figures with those for the smallest vertebrate – the dwarf goby. This minute fish from the Philippines is half an inch (13 mm) long. The smallest mammal, which is the Etruscan shrew, has a body that is only 2 inches (5 cm) long. It is a good deal smaller than many insects.

The **arrow-poison frog** is brilliantly colored and lives in Central and South America.

A

The **aardvark** escapes from its enemies by burrowing at lightning speed with its formidable digging claws.

Aardvark

The aardvark gets its name from the Afrikaans word meaning "earth pig." It is an African burrowing mammal with a stumpy, thickset body, a large snout, donkeylike ears, and a tough gray skin sparsely covered with coarse hair. The animal stands about 2 ft. (60 cm) high at the shoulder, and its tail, which tapers at the end, is about 2 ft. (60 cm) long. The feet have very strong digging claws – four on the front feet and five on the hind.

The aardvark is nocturnal and a TERMITE eater. With its powerful claws it can rip through the walls of termite nests that are difficult for a man to break with a pick. Having made a hole in the nest, the animal inserts its long slender tongue and laps up the insects.

The mouth contains 26 teeth, which are unusual in that they have no enamel or roots, and they continue to grow throughout the animal's life.

ORDER: Tubulidentata
FAMILY: Orycteropidae
SPECIES: *Orycteropus afer*

Aardwolf

The aardwolf is a member of the HYENA family, but has larger ears and weaker jaws than true hyenas. Its name is Afrikaans for "earth wolf." The aardwolf ranges through southern and eastern Africa, living mainly in sandy plains or bushy country. It spends the day in rock crevices or in a sleeping chamber at the end of a long burrow.

Aardwolves feed at night on insects which they sweep up with a long, tacky tongue. One aardwolf stomach was found to contain 40,000 termites. When insects are in short supply, mice, small birds, and eggs are eaten.

Aardwolves breed once a year. Each litter contains two to four young, born blind. The animal's enemies are PYTHONS, LIONS, and LEOPARDS. It defends itself by emitting a foul-smelling fluid from the anal glands.

ORDER: Carnivora
FAMILY: Hyaenidae
SPECIES: *Proteles cristatus*

Abalone

Abalones are sea snails related to the LIMPETS. They live in many coastal areas, especially in warmer regions. The body is little more than a muscular foot with a head at one end. The head carries a pair of eyes and sensory tentacles and a frill of tentacles surrounds the body. Water is drawn in beneath the shell and the oxygen is extracted as it passes over the gills. The water is then expelled through a line of holes which runs across the top of the shell.

Abalones avoid the light and come out at night to find food. They are vegetarians that crawl over rock faces and browse on seaweed. An abalone scrapes up its food with its *radula*, a tongue made up of large numbers of small horny teeth.

ORDER: Archaeogastropoda
FAMILY: Haliotidae
GENUS: *Haliotis*

Accentor

Accentors are small, sparrowlike birds found throughout Europe and Asia. Unlike SPARROWS, they have slender, finely pointed bills

and they are, in fact, more closely related to THRUSHES or WARBLERS. The two most common species are the dunnock, or hedge sparrow, and the alpine accentor, which is found from Spain to Japan. The latter is a larger, more brightly colored bird than the somber gray and brown dunnock, and has a whitish bib spotted with black.

Accentors usually live in mountainous regions, often well above the tree line. The alpine accentor is no exception, one race breeding at altitudes of up to 18,000 ft. (5,500 m). However, most accentors breed at lower levels, in scrub-type vegetation. The dunnock is particularly common in woods, hedgerows, and gardens. In summer accentors feed on insects; in winter, they live almost entirely on seeds and berries.

ORDER: Passeriformes
FAMILY: Prunellidae
GENUS: *Prunella*

The **addax** is a large antelope with a cattlelike appearance.

Acorn worm

There are about 70 species of acorn worms, ranging from about 20 to 76 in. (50 to 190 cm) in length. The body has three main parts, the front one is acorn shaped and known as the *proboscis*. A short, fleshy collar lies just behind the proboscis. The rest of the body is known as the trunk.

Acorn worms live on the seabed, from the shoreline down to depths of 10,000 ft. (3,050 m).

Each animal normally digs itself a U-shaped burrow and lives there with the proboscis sticking out of one opening. Water and debris is drawn in through the mouth, which is at the junction of the proboscis and the collar. The water then flows out through the gill slits, but food particles are passed further down the digestive tract. The sexes are separate. Eggs and sperm are merely shed into the water and fertilization occurs by chance. Most eggs are very small and they produce small *larvae* which swim freely in the plankton for a short while before settling on the seabed.

PHYLUM: Hemichordata
CLASS: Enteropneusta

Addax E

The addax, also known as the screwhorn antelope, is closely related to the ORYX. The addax's graceful, spiraling horns were prized by hunters. At one time the addax was common across the Sahara, but hunting and the des-

truction of its habitat have made it rare. Now, probably only about 6,000 live in the wild, but some have recently been bred in zoos. One young is born at a time, usually in winter or early spring. Adult males reach 40 in. (100 cm) at the shoulder and weigh around 250 lb. (113 kg). In winter, the body is grayish-brown, but it turns sandy or almost white in summer. The short, splayed hooves are adapted to journeys over desert sands. The addax can go for long periods without drinking water; it gets water from the plants it eats and from dew.

ORDER: Artiodactyla
FAMILY: Bovidae
SPECIES: *Addax nasomaculatus*

Adder

The adder belongs to the viper family. It has a short, fat body and a short tail. The record length is 32 in. (81 cm). Its color is gen-

Left: The **Alpine accentor** lives on rocky mountain slopes. Above: The **dunnock** resembles a house sparrow except for its slender beak.

erally a shade of brown, olive, gray, or cream with a dark zigzag line running down its back. The females can often be distinguished from the males because their color is more reddish, with darker red or brown markings.

Adders live in most of Europe and across Asia, and are the only snakes that live north of the Arctic Circle. They often bask in the sunshine on moors or hedgebanks and also live in marshy fields. They feed on LIZARDS, MICE, VOLES, and SHREWS. The young are born in August or September, and during the winter they *hibernate*. In northern Europe, hibernation lasts up to 275 days; in the south the winter sleep may take up as little as 105 days. Adder bites are poisonous to small animals but seldom fatal to human beings.

ORDER: Squamata
FAMILY: Viperidae
SPECIES: *Vipera berus*

The **adder**, or common viper of Europe, is easily recognized by its diamond-patterned back.

Aestivation

Shortage of water during hot, dry seasons causes some animals to hide away and go to sleep. This "summer sleep" is called aestivation. Desert animals, including frogs, toads, and some small rodents, avoid the heat and drought this way. So, too, do some reptiles. The African LUNGFISH burrows in the mud on the bed of its dried up river and waits until the water starts to flow again.

The **agouti**, a South American rodent, looks ratlike, but it is more closely related to the guinea pig.

Agouti

Agoutis are rodents that look a lot like long-legged GUINEA PIGS. Several species are found in Central and South America. They are mainly vegetarian, and like many other rodents, hoard food in small stores buried near landmarks. The agouti has many enemies. Although it makes its home in a shallow burrow, it prefers to escape by running away, often heading for the nearest river as it is a good swimmer. The agouti's slender build gives it great agility, and it can leap about 20 ft. (6 m) from a standing start. The agouti has become well adapted for running with its long legs and hooflike claws.

ORDER: Rodentia
FAMILY: Dasyproctidae
GENUS: *Dasyprocta*

Albatross   N, R, E

Albatrosses are large seabirds related to petrels. They have powerful hooked bills, stout bodies, and long, slender wings. The plumage of these birds is white with black parts or, in some species, brown. Albatrosses spend most of the time at sea, coming inland only to breed. They are expert gliders and can remain airborne for long periods. There are 13 species, 9 of which are only found in the Southern Hemisphere. They breed mainly on the Antarctic and oceanic islands. Another three species are found in the North Pacific, while the waved albatross breeds on the Galapagos Islands. The best known is the wandering albatross. It has a wingspan of over 12 ft. (3.7 m).

All species of albatross feed on marine life from the sea's surface, such as fish, squid, and crustaceans. They may live for 70 years. They do not breed until they are at least seven years old. Breeding grounds are usually on cliff tops, where the birds can take off easily. The albatross became well known through Coleridge's "Rhyme of the Ancient Mariner" as the bird of ill omen.

ORDER: Procellariiformes
FAMILY: Diomedeidae
GENUS: *Diomedea*

An **albatross** in flight; the bird spends most of its life soaring effortlessly over the vast oceans.

Alderfly

There are many species of alderflies. They are compact, dark-bodied and dark-winged relatives of the LACEWINGS. They fly poorly and are rarely found far from the still or slow moving water in which they spend their early lives. The *larvae* live in mud and silt and feed on other small animals. They have a feathery appearance, due to numerous external gills on the abdomen. They spend about a year in the water, and then pupate in debris at the water's edge. The adults may take nectar from flowers, but are most often seen just sitting on waterside plants. The females lay large clusters of eggs on leaves which hang over the water.

ORDER: Neuroptera
FAMILY: Sialidae

The **alderfly** is a poor flier.

Alewife

The alewife is a food fish of North America. It spawns in lakes and rivers from the St. Lawrence Seaway southward. As an ocean fish it is about 12 in. (30 cm) long when fully grown. In appearance, the alewife resembles its relatives the HERRING and the SHAD. When good catches are made, large quantities of the fish may be ground up to make fertilizer.

ORDER: Clupeiformes
FAMILY: Clupeidae
SPECIES: *Pomobolus pseudoharengus*

Alligator   N, E

Alligators are large, scaly reptiles that live on the banks of rivers and in the water. There are two species: the American alligator and the endangered Chinese alligator. The American alligator is the larger of the two, the record length being 19.16 ft. (5.84 m). American alligators live in the southeastern United States. Chinese alligators are found only in the Yangtze River basin. Alligators eat fish, small mammals, and birds. Each adult female lays 15 to 80 eggs in a nest mound she has made from mud and rotting vegetation. The heat produced by this decaying process helps to hatch the eggs two to three months later. Meanwhile the female stays close by. Then she removes the vegetation to help her hatchlings get out.

Alligators are similar to CROCODILES. The main difference between the crocodiles and alligators

The **American alligator** can be as large and as dangerous as a crocodile.

is in the teeth. When an alligator's mouth is shut, the upper teeth lie outside the lower teeth with its fourth lower tooth hidden in a pit in the upper jaw. With crocodiles, the teeth in the upper and lower jaws are in line and the fourth lower tooth is visible when the jaws are closed. An alligator also has a broader, shorter head and a blunter snout than a crocodile.

ORDER: Crocodilia
FAMILY: Alligatoridae
SPECIES: American: *Alligator mississippiensis*; Chinese: *Alligator sinensis*

Alpaca

The alpaca lives in the mountains of Peru, Bolivia, and Chile at altitudes between 7,900 and 11,800 ft. (2,400 and 3,600 m) above sea level. It is closely related to the LLAMA, which it resembles, but is smaller, being less than 5 ft. (150 cm) at the shoulder.

The alpaca's fleece, which may be black, white, or brown, grows between 8 and 16 in. (20 and 40 cm) long. It is finer and straighter than that of any other animal and alpacas are reared for this fine wool.

ORDER: Artiodactyla
FAMILY: Camelidae
SPECIES: *Lama pacos*

Amoeba

The amoebae are minute single-celled animals. The majority of species are less than .02 in. (.5 mm) across, although some reach .12 in. (3 mm) in diameter. The animals have no fixed shape and they continually push out "arms" in various directions. The protoplasm which makes up the bulk of the cell flows into one of the "arms." The whole animal thus moves forward.

Most species live in water, but some occur in damp soil and some live as parasites inside other animals. The typical amoeba feeds by engulfing other small organisms with its arms and digesting them. Amoebae normally reproduce simply by splitting into two halves,

but when the water becomes cold or begins to dry up an amoeba can form a tough wall around itself and go into a dormant state. When favorable conditions return, the wall breaks down and out come not one but dozens of tiny amoebae to repopulate the pond.

PHYLUM: Protozoa
CLASS: Sarcodina

Amphibians

The Class Amphibia is represented by about 4,000 species of *carnivorous* animals arranged in three distinct groups. These are the frogs and toads, the newts and salamanders, and the caecilians.

The amphibians evolved from some kind of lobe-finned fish about 400 million years ago, and today's amphibians are very different from the ancestral forms. They have not really broken away from the water, however, for they lack waterproof skins and they can survive only in moist conditions. Most of them have to return to the water to breed. But some species spend all their lives in the water, and some have become fully land living by giving birth to miniature adults instead of laying eggs in the water.

Amphipod

The name given to more than 4,500 species of small crustaceans ranging in size from more than 1 in. (25 mm) to less than .04 in. (1 mm) in length. Their bodies are compressed from side to side, and the backs are curved in an arc when at rest. They have many pairs of legs. Those on the front part of the body are used for walking and those on the rear part for swimming. Most amphipods live in the sea, but some are found in fresh water or on land. They are scavengers, feeding on any kind of

The **alpaca's** handsome brown coat keeps it warm in the cold air of the Andes Mountains.

Left: An **amphipod** – the freshwater shrimp Gammarus, enlarged 5 times.

dead plant or animal matter. The so-called freshwater shrimp and a number of sea species belong to the genus *Gammarus*. The males are often seen carrying the females under their bodies.

ORDER: Amphipoda

Amphisbaena

Amphisbaenids, or worm lizards, are a strange family of reptiles which spend most of their lives underground, coming to the surface only at night or after heavy rain. Their bodies are well adapted for burrowing, most species having lost all trace of limbs, and their eyes are small. Their bodies are covered with scales arranged in rings, so at first glance they look like earthworms. The head and tail are often blunt and hard to tell apart. This helped to give the animals their name, which means "coming both ways." People used to think that each end of an amphisbaena had a head. Amphisbaenids live mainly in tropical lands and feed on ANTS and other insects.

ORDER: Squamata
FAMILY: Amphisbaenidae

The **anaconda** is one of the world's largest and heaviest snakes. It can swallow whole animals over 1 yd. (1 m) long.

Anaconda

This name usually describes the water boa, one of the world's largest snakes. It lives in much of tropical South America east of the Andes. It is said to grow longer than 30 ft. (9 m), and only the reticulated PYTHON rivals it for size.

Anacondas are olive green with large, round, black spots along the body. They seldom wander far from water, by day resting in pools or sluggish streams, or sunbathing on low branches over water. There they lie in wait for DEER, PECCARIES, fish, and other animals. Anacondas kill either by drowning their prey or by constricting it with their long coils until the victim suffocates.

Like other boas, anacondas give birth to live young instead of laying eggs. One female will produce 20 to 40, even as many as 100, young at a time. Each young is up to 1 yd. (1 m) long.

ORDER: Squamata
FAMILY: Boidae
SPECIES: *Eunectes murinus*

The **anchovy** feeds on surface plankton.

Anchovy

The name given to about 100 species of small food fish related to the HERRING. These live in vast schools in tropical and temperate seas and are also common in bays and estuaries. Besides being an important source of human food, anchovies are a favorite prey of the great TUNAS and of seabirds. Their maximum size is about 8 in. (20 cm).

ORDER: Clupeiformes
FAMILY: Clupeidae

Angelfish

Freshwater fish, common in tropical aquariums. Marine angelfish are very similar, narrow-bodied bony fish having equally

Angelfish

Angelfish are favorites in the aquarium. The angelfish above is the original natural silver fish. The black and gold fish is a small Pacific variety. The imperial fish can be 16 in. (40 cm) long.

Black and gold angelfish

Imperial angelfish

brilliant colors. Both types get the name angelfish from their delicate bodies and winglike or flaplike *pectoral fins*. Angelfish can be observed in aquariums displaying their colors, advertizing their territorial rights, and telling other members of their species to keep away.

Angelfish range in length from 2 to 24 in. (5 to 60 cm). They feed on small water animals, picking these up with a small mouth which contains many crushing teeth. Some have slender snouts for sucking prey out from crevices.

ORDER: Perciformes
FAMILIES: Chaetodontidae and Pomocanthidae (marine); Cichlidae (freshwater)

Anglerfish

Any one of 350 or more species of strange-looking fish, all of which catch their prey by angling with a rod and line. This rod is really an extension of a spine or ray of the *dorsal fin*. The squat, ugly bodies of anglerfish are explained by their sedentary way of life. Because they remain quite still, angling, for most of the time, they have no need for the streamlining which goes with fast swimming.

Anglerfish fall into two groups. One group is drab in color and the bodies of the anglers are often covered with flaps of skin, very like the seaweed in which the fish are to be found. The other group, the deep-sea anglers, are generally black in color, which conceals their bodies in the dark depths where they live. However, their fishing line is often luminous, to attract unsuspecting prey.

The **angwantibo** was unknown to Europeans until 1860, when it was discovered in the Cameroons.

In four species of these fish the much smaller male fish attaches himself to the female's body with his jaws and his body eventually fuses with hers to share the same blood system. This attachment of the male ensures fertilization of the female anglerfish, who might otherwise have to wait a very long time in the inky vastness before meeting another male.

ORDER: Lophiiformes
FAMILY: Various

Angwantibo

The angwantibo is a rare animal which looks like a cross between a kitten and a BUSHBABY. The name probably comes from a West African word, "angwan," which means cat. One subspecies has soft, thick fur which is yellowish-brown or fawn with whitish underparts. The other subspecies is generally golden-red, with grayish underparts. The angwantibo lives in Africa, between the lower Niger and Zaire Rivers. This agile animal lives in tall trees. It is active at night and little is known of its habits.

ORDER: Primates
FAMILY: Lorisidae
SPECIES: *Arctocebus calabarensis*

Ani

The anis are a subfamily of the cuckoos, though they do not lay their eggs in the nests of other birds as many cuckoos do. Anis are about 15 in. (38 cm) long, and range from the southern borders of the United States to Argentina. They live in flocks and often follow other animals to feed on the insects driven out by their approach. Each flock numbers from 7 to 15 birds, often mostly males. The flock occupies a territory that it defends against neighboring flocks of anis. The territory contains separate areas for roosting, nesting, and feeding.

ORDER: Cuculiformes
FAMILY: Cuculidae
SPECIES: *Crotophaga*

Animal Language

Animals use sounds and gestures to communicate, just as people do. But they also use the sense of touch and the sense of smell, senses that are developed only partly in man. Animal language is limited in what it can convey. The principal messages concern danger, the location of food, the ownership of territory, and the urge to mate. Other signals help to keep families and groups together.

Bird song is one of the most familiar sounds in the animal world. A bird's song in the spring may convey either or both of two messages – "This is my territory, keep off," or, "I want a mate." Birds that flock together, such as rooks or starlings, often "chatter" in a companionable way. Birds have certain calls that they use for keeping in touch, for example, mother birds and their young call to each other. Such call sounds are apparently instinctive. So are many of the warning notes such as the "alarm call" of the blackbird. But birds learn some songs only by imitating their parents.

Mammals use sound a great deal, too. A domestic cat purrs to show that it is pleased and snarls and spits when it is afraid or angry. Cats have learned to meow when they want to be let out or be fed. Here, cats are using language to communicate with humans. This use of language between different species is unusual. In the wild, wolves howl to signal to each other. There is also a pack howl which is a kind of "get-together" signal. During a pack howl the wolves wag their tails and appear friendly and excited toward one another. When hunting they communicate with short sharp barks.

Fish also communicate by sounds. The grunting noises made by catfish apparently serve as call signals to keep a school together in darkness. Other fish appear to make sounds that help them to find mates. Mammals that live in the sea, such as whales and dolphins (which are among the most intelligent animals), also make a variety of noises. Scientists do not yet know exactly what these signals convey.

Gestures and action play a great part in the language of animals. Male fiddler crabs wave their giant claws to attract females in a gesture that is just like our beckoning. Rabbits signal the approach of danger by thumping on the ground with their long hind legs. Ants communicate by touching their antennae.

Possibly the most elaborate system of communication by gestures is that made by honeybees. A worker bee that has found a source of nectar or pollen performs a kind of dance in front of her fellow workers to let them know where the source is. If it is near the hive she does a round dance; if it is farther away she performs a figure eight, wagging her tail. The speed of the dance conveys very accurately the distance of the food. The direction of part of the dance indicates the direction from the hive.

Animals use scent for communicating much more than people do. A dog, for example, leaves it own scent on trees and other objects in order to mark out its territory. Fish and other animals release some chemical substances when they are hurt or frightened. Other animals of the same species scent danger and keep away. Fish such as minnows that are hunted by pike can smell their enemies at a distance. In the insect world smells are very important. Ants leave a chemical trail behind them which other ants can follow. Scent also plays a great part in courtship. Male and female fish are guided to each other by it, and tests have shown that the scent of a female moth will lure males from considerable distances.

The greylag goose communicates different emotions by standing in different positions. The top bird is about to attack, the other is on the defense.

When a bee finds nectar, it dances to tell the other bees where the nectar is. The direction of the dance shows where the source is in relation to the hive.

Annelids

This animal phylum contains the segmented worms – long animals whose bodies are clearly organized in rings, or segments. There are about 9,000 species, including earthworms, leeches, and the numerous forms of BRISTLE-WORMS that swim in the sea and burrow in the seabed. These animals fall into three distinct classes.

Earthworms look quite smooth, but nearly every segment actually bears four pairs of small bristles on its lower surface which give the animal a good grip on the sides of its tunnels. Earthworms are *hermaphrodite*, meaning that each individual has both male and female organs, but they have to pair up before they can lay their eggs.

Leeches have no bristles, but there is a powerful sucker at each end of the body. Most leeches live in fresh water and they are hermaphrodite.

Bristleworms have numerous bristles on lobes extending from nearly every segment. Apart from a few river species, they all live in the sea, but they are very variable in shapes and habits. Unlike the other annelids, the bristleworms usually have separate sexes.

Leafcutter ants cut pieces of leaves and carry them to their nests. They feed on mold which they grow on pulped leaves.

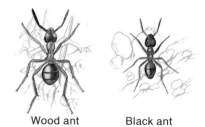

Wood ant   Black ant

A **wood ants'** nest cut open to show different rooms. The ants obtain honeydew from aphids by stroking them with their antennae.

Anoa   E

Two species of small, wild cattle found only in Sulawesi (Celebes) in Indonesia, They are also called dwarf buffalo. The mountain anoa is the smaller of the two species, standing 2 to 3 ft. (60 to 90 cm) at the shoulder. The lowland anoa is nearly 3.5 ft. (107 cm) high. Anoa have straight, conical, backward-pointing horns up to 1 ft. (30 cm) long. These brown or black animals have always been treated as two species, but some experts now think that they may be varieties of the same species. Because of hunting, the cutting down of mountain forests, and the draining of lowland swamps, the numbers of anoa have been much reduced. There is a danger that they may become extinct.

ORDER: Artiodactyla
FAMILY: Bovidae
SPECIES: Mountain: *Anoa anoa*; lowland: *Anoa depressicornis*

Ant

The ants are an immense family of insects, with about 15,000 species, belonging to the same order as the BEES and WASPS. They vary a great deal in size, but can always be recognized by their elbowed antennae and the slender waist which bears one or two distinct bulges. The females of many species can defend themselves with stingers, and those that lack stingers can often fire acid at their attackers. As in bees and wasps, the males do not have a stinger.

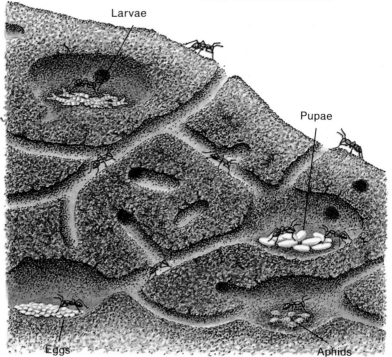

Larvae

Pupae

Eggs

Aphids

All ant species are social, living in colonies containing anything from a few dozen to several million individuals. Each colony is ruled by one or more queens, but the great bulk of the population consists of workers. These are sterile females which never grow wings. Some workers may be larger than others and have much bigger jaws. These are called soldiers, and their job is to defend the colony. Not all ant species have soldiers.

The queens of most species have

Ants bring cocoons to a spot where the Sun's warmth can speed up development.

wings when they first mature, and many fly out in great mating swarms, but they break off their wings before rejoining the colony or starting a new one. Male ants, also winged, only appear at certain times of the year – just in time for the mating flights. The males are produced from unfertilized eggs laid by the queens. New queens

and workers develop from fertilized eggs, but grubs destined to be queens receive more food and thus grow much bigger.

The ARMY ANTS have no settled home, but other ant species all have some kind of nest. Species with small colonies may nest in hollow plant stems, while WEAVER ANTS nest in pouches formed by binding several leaves together. Many tropical ants build nests in the trees, using soil and chewed wood mixed with saliva as their

building material. The most common types of nest, however, are in the ground. Soil is dug out to form underground chambers, and the ants usually make use of the mounds of excavated soil as well.

Ant nests have none of the elaborate cell architecture found in the nests of the social wasps and the honeybee, but the larger nests are efficiently organized. Each of the numerous chambers has a particular use and may be a nursery, a pantry, a yard, or even a cemetery. In the center of the nest there is a royal chamber in which the queen lays her eggs. She is constantly tended by workers, and as long as she remains in good health the colony runs very smoothly. Workers take the eggs to hatchery chambers, and may move the larvae again when they hatch. The larvae are fed by the workers, and when fully grown they spin silken cocoons around themselves. These cocoons, which are often sold as

"ant eggs" in pet shops, are usually taken to a chamber near the surface of the nest. There the Sun's warmth can speed up the development of the adults.

After mating, a queen may enter an existing colony – often her original home – or she may start a new one. In starting a new colony, the queen generally secretes herself in the ground, lays a few eggs, and rears a few small workers by feeding them on further eggs. These workers then begin building the nest.

There is another method of starting a colony. In this, the new queen enters the nest of another species. She lays eggs there, and the hosts rear her young. After a while she displaces the original queen, and the colony gradually becomes populated entirely with the invading queen's offspring.

A number of species are unable to rear enough workers for their needs and they overcome this

problem by taking slaves. They raid the nests of other ants and steal pupae. The ants emerging from these pupae become workers in the nests of their captors.

The army ants and some other species are pure carnivores, eating nothing but the flesh of other animals. We can call these species hunting ants. There are also a number of harvesting ants, which feed mainly on seeds. These ants inhabit relatively dry areas and can be seen dragging seeds into their nests from all directions. The leafcutter ants of tropical Ameria actually grow their own food. They cut pieces of leaves from the plants and carry them to their nests where they chew them to pulp. The pulp is then spread out in the chambers and mold grows on it. The ants eat nothing but this mold. Most ants, however, are omnivorous, eating fruit and various small animals. Honeydew from APHIDS is another favorite food, and some ants actually herd the aphids as people herd cows. They use their jaws and stingers to protect the aphids from various enemies, and even carry aphids into their nests and install them on roots passing through the chambers.

ORDER: Hymenoptera
FAMILY: Formicidae

Antbird

A family of 221 species of birds found in central and northern South America and also on Trinidad and Tobago. They live in lowland thickets and forests and on mountain ranges, but never in open country. All are fairly small, ranging in size from around 3.5 to 14 in. (9 to 36 cm) in length. Their beaks are usually hooked and their plumage is generally dull, with patches of black and white. In many species there is a marked difference between the sexes. Most feed on insects and small snails, and not especially on ants.

ORDER: Passeriformes
FAMILY: Formicariidae

Anteater N, V

Anteaters are found in Central and South America. They eat many kinds of insects, but generally feed on ANTS and TERMITES. An anteater uses the sharp claws of its forefeet to tear a hole in the wall of a termite nest, pushes its muzzle inside, and laps up the inhabitants by means of a sticky saliva on its 8 to 10 in. (20 to 25 cm) tongue.

There are three South American species. The giant anteater is of a startling appearance. Its long, cylindrical snout is balanced by a bushy tail. Its front feet face one another, the formidable claws folded inward so that the animal walks on its knuckles The hind feet, however, stand flat on the ground. From nose to rump, the giant anteater is 3 to 4 ft. (90 to 122 cm) long. Its tail adds another 2 to 3 ft. (60 to 90 cm). Its hair is coarse and stiff, gray-brown on the head and body, becoming darker on the hindquarters and tail. Across the shoulders, wedge-shaped black stripes bordered with white effectively camouflage the animal by breaking up its outline.

The giant anteater lives in the swamps, grasslands, and open forests from Belize and Guatemala to northern Argentina. It spends most of its life in a search for food, shuffling around with its nose to the ground.

Female giant anteaters have single offspring. The young are probably born in spring after a gestation period of 190 days. The baby stays with its mother until she is pregnant again, traveling easily by clinging to her back.

The silky or two-toed anteater and the tamandua have shorter snouts and lack the giant anteater's plume of hair on their tails. All of the anteaters manage to eat without teeth. The silky anteater is named for the soft texture of its coat. It is squirrel-sized with a long *prehensile* tail. The tamandua, too, has a prehensile tail which lacks fur. The body fur is usually tan with a black "vest."

ORDER: Edentata
FAMILY: Myrmecophagidae
SPECIES: Giant: *Myrmecophaga tridactyla*; silky (two-toed): *Cyclopes didactylus*; tamandua: *Tamandua tetradactyla*

The **giant anteater's** front feet are turned inward so that the animal walks on its knuckles.

Antelope

Antelopes belong to the same family as CATTLE, GOATS, and SHEEP. They are mostly delicate and timid creatures, capable of running at great speed on their slender legs when threatened by

A large male waterbuck; these **antelopes** are native to most parts of Africa south of the Sahara.

predators. A few species live in Asia, including the SAIGA of central Asia, various GAZELLES in the deserts of southwest Asia, and the BLACKBUCK and NILGAI of India. There are no true antelopes in the Americas, although one North American animal is called the PRONGHORN antelope. But this animal belongs to a different, ancient family that arose and developed in North America.

Africa has the greatest number of species and the largest populations of antelopes, many of which can be seen in huge herds, particularly in some of the magnificent national parks. There are 72 African species in all, and they occur throughout the continent, as they are adapted to many kinds of habitats. For example, the endangered ADDAX is adapted to the life in deserts, and some antelopes, like the bongo, live in forests. Others live on mountainsides and a few, such as the WATERBUCK, prefer marshes. Some species, such as the lechwe, may spend all day submerged in water up to their necks in flooded grassland. However, most antelopes are found on the *savanna* of eastern and south-ern Africa. Antelopes vary in size from the tiny DIK-DIK, DUIKER, SUNI, and royal antelope to the massive giant ELAND, the largest of all antelopes. The difference in size is caused by adaptation to environment, as is the varying diet of antelopes. Because of special adaptations, various antelopes and other aimals can live side by side without competition over the same food. They graze and browse on a very wide range of plants, and where two species feed on one type of plant they usually eat different parts of it.

Nearly all antelopes have horns. Females may be horned, but their

Kudu and **springbok antelopes** drinking at a Namibian water hole.

horns are mostly smaller than those of the males. Horns may be short and straight or long and elaborately curved, sometimes in an elegant spiral, but they are never forked like the antlers of DEER. The horns are sometimes interlocked in combats between males at the mating season or in the defense of territory. The fight then becomes a pushing contest. But sharp, pointed horns may be used as weapons. The ORYX have speared lions with their horns and BUSHBUCK have been known to kill men. The coats of antelopes are mostly smooth. Many colors and patterns occur, although brown and gray are the most common colors.

Because of their attractive horns, their edible meat, and useful skins, several species of antelope have been overhunted and are threatened with extinction. Only a few hundred of the magnificent giant SABLE ANTELOPE of Angola have survived. They are now being protected.

ORDER: Artiodactyla
FAMILY: Bovidae

Antlion

Adult antlions are mostly large insects related to the LACEWINGS. They could be confused with DRAGONFLIES at first sight, but they fly much more slowly and have much larger, clubbed antennae. These insects are found mainly in the tropics, although some species live in Europe – especially in southern areas. Several species occur in the United States.

Antlions get their name from the habits of the larvae, which feed on ANTS and other small insects. Some larvae live freely on the ground, but the best known make little pits in sandy soil. These larvae bury themselves at the bottom of their pits, with just their great jaws above the sand, and wait for their prey to tumble in. The larvae are often called doodlebugs in the United States.

ORDER: Neuroptera
FAMILY: Myrmeleontidae

Aphid

The aphids are also known as plant lice. They are small, sap-sucking bugs that do great harm to many crops and other plants. Familiar examples include the blackfly, which attacks beans and spinach, and various species of

The **antlion larva** has fearsome jaws with which it grabs its prey.

greenfly which infest roses. The insects have pear-shaped bodies, with or without wings, and small heads with a slender beak which pierces the plant tissues. The hind end of the body usually has a pair of horns, called *cornicles*, which give off waxy and pungent secretions. These horns protect the

Apes

Apes are the monkeylike animals that are nearest to humans in structure and development. For this reason they are called anthropoid – "man-like." It was once thought that humans were descended from the apes, but it now seems certain that apes and humans as we know them today had a common ancestor.

Two of the four kinds of apes – the orangutan and the gibbon – live in Asia. The other two – the chimpanzee and the gorilla – live in Africa. Remains of the earliest Hominids – the group that includes both apes and human beings – have been found in these two continents.

The apes resemble humans in that they have no tail and in walking upright some of the time. Their brains are much better developed than those of other primates. Most of the bones, muscles, nerves, and other internal organs of apes are very similar to those of humans. Apes have shorter legs and longer arms than human beings and their big toes are more thumblike.

Skeletons of man and **ape**. The ape's arms are longer than its legs and the pelvic girdle (stippled) has developed to suit the different postures.

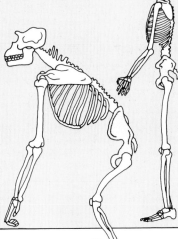

aphids from some of their enemies, although they do not deter the LADYBUGS and LACEWINGS. Aphids are rarely more than a tenth of an inch (3 mm) long. They live on roots, stems, and leaves, and, as well as merely removing sap from the plants, also carry serious viral diseases. Large aphid populations may cause leaves to curl up, and some species cause the formation of growths, called *galls*.

Many aphids have complicated life histories, and this is particularly true of those living in cool climates. The blackfly, for example, passes the winter in the egg stage on various shrubs. The eggs hatch in spring and the resulting insects are all wingless females. These reproduce without mating – a phenomenon known as *parthenogenesis* – and bring forth active young at the rate of several each day. These youngsters, again all female, are soon reproducing themselves, and winged individuals begin to appear. These fly to the beans and other host plants and continue to reproduce at a rapid rate. Great populations of winged and wingless aphids thus develop on the plants. The winged forms can move around and spread the infestation over a wide area. Male aphids appear later in the summer. They mate with certain females, which then lay the winter eggs on the shrubs.

The sap on which the aphids feed is very rich in sugar, but contains little protein. In order to get enough protein, the aphids have to take in way too much sugar, but they simply pass the excess sugar out again at the hind end in the form of a sweet liquid called honeydew. The leaves of many trees become sticky with honeydew in the summer. Ants are very fond of sweet things and they regularly stroke the aphids to make them give out honeydew. Some ants actually guard the aphid colonies, and may even take aphids into their nests to protect them.
ORDER: Hemiptera-Homoptera

Green aphids cluster on a rose shoot to drink its sap through their long, piercing beaks.

Apollo butterfly R, E, Ex

The beautiful apollo butterfly, which is related to the SWALLOWTAIL, flies in the mountainous parts of Europe and Asia. Throughout the summer it can be seen floating elegantly from flower to flower or sunning itself on the ground. Its dark, hairy body helps to absorb heat in the cool climate. The caterpillar feeds on saxifrage and other alpine plants and, unlike most butterfly *larvae*, spins a *cocoon* in which to pupate. The butterfly is not found above about 6,000 ft. (1,800 m), but related species occur higher up in the Alps and in other mountain ranges in Asia and North America.
ORDER: Lepidoptera
FAMILY: Papilionidae
SPECIES: *Parnassius apollo*

Apollo butterflies are found in many parts of the world, usually in high places.

Arachnids

The Class Arachnida contains the SPIDERS, SCORPIONS, MITES, TICKS, and a few other groups on land and in the sea. There are usually four pairs of walking legs, and the animals lack *antennae* and wings. Some mites suck plant sap, and the ticks are bloodsuckers, but most arachnids are *carnivores*, despite the fact that they have no real jaws.

The garden spider is one of the most often-seen **arachnids**.

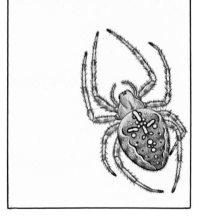

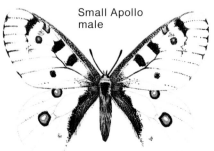

Small Apollo male

Clouded Apollo male

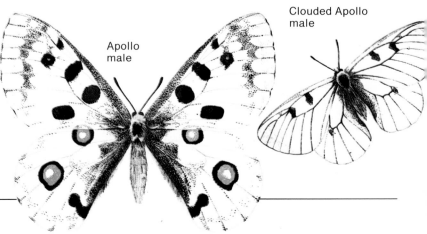

Apollo male

Arapaima

One of the largest of all freshwater fish, the arapaima grows up to 15 ft. (4.6 m) in length and 440 lb. (200 kg) in weight. It lives in shallow waters of rivers of northern South America. It has an ancestry going back 100 million years without much change, and can be regarded as a living fossil.

Among the primitive features of the arapaima is the way it uses its *swim bladder* as a lung, rising to the surface every now and then to take a gulp of air. This feature is most probably an adaptation toward survival in drought conditions, similar to the adaptations of the LUNGFISH.

Arapaimas eat anything from worms, snails, and weeds, to fish of medium size.

ORDER: Osteoglossiformes
FAMILY: Osteoglossidae
SPECIES: *Arapaima gigas*

Archerfish

A group of freshwater or slightly saltwater fish which shoot down their insect prey with well-aimed drops of water. There are five species, living in rivers and mangrove swamps from India through Southeast Asia to the northern shore of Australia.

Archerfish mainly feed on small water creatures swimming or floating near the surface. But from time to time they rise to the surface and spit a trail of water droplets which can bring down insects. These insects can be crawling on leaves or stems, as far away as 6.5 ft. (2 m). At the moment of shooting the tip of the snout just breaks the water but the fish's eyes remain submerged. A sudden, powerful movement of the archerfish's gill covers pumps water through the gills into the mouth. At the same time the fish raises its tongue to convert a groove in the roof of its mouth into a narrow tube, through which the water is driven at high speed. Archerfish begin to shoot at prey in this manner when they are still very young and small in size. As they grow, their range and accuracy increase.

ORDER: Perciformes
FAMILY: Toxotidae

Arctic fox

The Arctic fox is similar to the red fox, but is smaller, with smaller ears which help to retain heat. It lives in the *tundra* regions of Europe, Asia, North America, and Greenland. In winter its thick

Archerfish capture insects by shooting out jets of water. The tongue and roof of the fish's mouth form the equivalent of a gun barrel.

Arctic fox change color with the seasons.

white coat provides it with insulation and camouflage in the snow. In summer its coat is grayish-yellow with white underparts. Hairs on the soles of its feet give the fox a good grip on snow and ice.

Arctic fox live in small groups and eat a wide variety of food. In winter, food is difficult to find and they follow POLAR BEARS to take advantage of any uneaten seal meat. In summer, however, food is more plentiful. They catch birds, such as gulls and ducks, and mammals, such as voles and hares. In Europe, LEMMINGS are the main source of food and the population of fox rises and falls with the explosive rise and fall of lemming populations.

Breeding begins in April and five to eight cubs are born in May or June. However, when lemmings are abundant, as many as 20 cubs may be born in the same litter. A second litter is born in July or August.

ORDER: Carnivora
FAMILY: Canidae
SPECIES: *Alopex lagopus*

Armadillo   N, V

The name armadillo means "little armored thing" in Spanish, which refers to the animal's *carapace*, or body armor. The carapace is unusual in that it is made up of

The **three-banded armadillo** has bony plates that give the animal a formidable defense. It can also protect itself by curling into a ball.

small plates of bone rather than of compressed hair or *keratin*. This gives this fast-moving animal a formidable defense. The three-banded armadillo, or apara, is additionally protected by its ability to roll into a ball. When forced to swim, the weight of its carapace would be a disadvantage except that the armadillo has developed an inflatable intestine which gives it added bouyancy.

Armadillos, of which there are 20 species, are found only in the Americas. The largest is the giant armadillo of the rain forest of eastern South America. The giant's 3 ft. (90 cm) body can weigh up to 130 lb. (59 kg). It has up to 100 small teeth, more than double the number found in most other mammals. The smallest species is only 6 in. (15 cm) long.

Most armadillos are nocturnal and live in burrows one yard (1 m) beneath the surface. They are omnivorous, living on insects, snakes, and lizards as well as plants. The armadillo uses its sicklelike claws to dig into ant and termite runs, extracting the insects with its long, extendible tongue.
ORDER: Edentata
FAMILY: Dasypodidae

Armored catfish

The name given to any one of 30 species of South American catfish, with *barbels*, or whiskers which give them their name. All these small stream-dwellers are remarkable for the bony armor which clothes their bodies. They are for the most part, bottom dwellers, feeding on small animals and fallen carrion found in the mud. Their armor is protective against attack by other fish. One species, the talking catfish, is the most heavily armored of all fish, being covered with bony plates and spines.
ORDER: Siluriformes
FAMILY: Doradidae (thorny catfish); Callichthyidae (mailed catfish)

Army ant

The army ants, also called driver or legionary ants, are ants that have no permanent homes, although, like all ants, they live in colonies. Some colonies contain millions of individuals. There are several different species, scattered through most of the tropical regions. They are all fiercely carnivorous and they eat almost any kind of animal that cannot escape from their marching columns. Even a horse will be killed and stripped to a skeleton by some of the African species if it is tethered in their path, but the usual prey are insects and other small animals.

At night, the worker ants cluster together to form a dense mass, sometimes as much as a yard (1 m) across. Their legs are intertwined, and their bodies form a living nest for the queen and youngsters in the center. This temporary home is called a bivouac. At daybreak, the workers stream out to forage, and their columns look like ropes snaking over the ground. The large-jawed soldiers march along on the outside of the columns to protect them. The columns usually fan out after a while and cover a wide area. Prey is torn to pieces when caught, and stored along the route. The ants collect it as they return to the bivouac later in the day.

Toward dusk they stream out again carrying the larvae. The queen moves with them on this occasion and they settle into a new bivouac perhaps 100 yd. (100 m) away, ready to hunt over a new area the next day. The queen has distinct periods of egg laying, and when she is ready to lay, the colony becomes more settled. A bivouac may then last for three weeks or more, and the ants go out from the same place each day. But as soon as the eggs hatch the ants become nomadic again, because they need extra food for the larvae and would soon exhaust one area. The queens are much larger than the workers, and wingless. Males are also very large – up to 2 in. (5 cm) long – and they have wings. They are sometimes known as sausage flies because of their shape.
ORDER: Hymenoptera
FAMILY: Formicidae

Arrow-poison frog

Arrow-poison frogs secrete a powerful poison which can cause instant death. The frogs are found only in Central and South America, where Indians have long extracted the poison from their bodies to use on arrowheads.

The **arrow-poison frog** secretes a powerful poison from its skin.

Many species are brilliantly colored. The strawberry arrow-poison frog is red and black. Another kind is yellow with stripes of black running lengthwise down the head and body and around the limbs. A Cuban member of the family, is the smallest frog in the world, measuring less than half an inch (1.3 cm).
ORDER: Salientia
FAMILY: Dendrobatidae

Arrowworm

This name applies to 65 species of tiny, transparent animals that form part of the PLANKTON. Arrowworms vary from .8 to 4 in. (2 to 10 cm) in length. Their bodies are divided into three sections; a short head, a long trunk, and a short tail. They are very difficult to see, except for their black eyes and any food they may have swallowed. They eat other small animals and larvae in the plankton. Each individual contains both male and female organs.
PHYLUM: Chaetognatha

Asp

The asp is a snake in the same family as the ADDER. Their colors are rather similar, but the asp's back is often marked with dark slanting bars, and a streak down

Arthropods

This is the largest of all the animal phyla. It contains more species than all the other phyla put together. There are very nearly a million known species. The name of the phylum means "jointed foot" and refers to the clearly jointed appearance of the limbs. The body is also clearly segmented in most arthropods, and it seems certain that the arthropods evolved from some kind of ANNELID ancestor that developed legs. All arthropods have a tough, and often very hard coat, or *exoskeleton*. This does not grow with the animal and all arthropods must *molt* at intervals. The old coat is shed and a new coat is formed underneath.

The arthropods include CENTIPEDES, MILLIPEDES, SHRIMP, CRABS, all the INSECTS, SPIDERS, and SCORPIONS.

Flat-backed millipede

Sandhopper

Shore crab

Marsh fritillary

Great diving beetle

Grasshopper

the middle. Also, the asp's snout is turned up, unlike the adder's.

The asp is common in many parts of Europe, usually farther south than the adder. Asps like wasteland, hedges, and scrub. Some have been found high up in the Alps. They are slow moving but aggressive and more dangerous to people than adders; their bite can be fatal.
ORDER: Squamata
FAMILY: Viperidae
SPECIES: *Vipera aspis*

The **asp** is more aggressive and dangerous than its close relative, the **adder**.

Ass

There are two species of wild asses. The North African ass probably gave rise to the domestic DONKEY. Asses stand 3 to 4.5 ft. (.9 to 1.4 m) high at the shoulder and have a gray or brownish coat. The legs are often striped and the ears long. Mules are the offspring of female horses and male asses. The parents of the rarer hinny are a female ass and a male horse. Both *hybrids* are sterile. Wild asses live in desert or semidesert areas, sometimes on plains, but more often in hilly regions. These wary animals live in troops of 10 to 12, consisting of a stallion, several females, and some young. Courtship takes place in the spring or early summer and the foals are born 11 to 12 months later. Man is the wild ass's main enemy, and WOLVES attack solitary animals.

ORDER: Perissodactyla
FAMILY: Equidae
SPECIES: North African: *Equus asinus*; Central Asian: *Equus hemionus*

Assassin Bug

The assassin bugs, of which there are more than 3,000 species, are predators that feed mainly on other insects. Reaching lengths of 1.5 in. (4 cm) or more, they are generally stoutly built, but some are very slender. Assassin bugs often resemble the insects on which they feed. They usually grasp prey in their front legs, and then plunge their long, curved beaks in to suck out the juices.

ORDER: Hemiptera-Heteroptera
FAMILY: Reduviidae

Atlas moth

With a wingspan reaching 10 in. (25 cm), the atlas moth is one of the world's largest moths. It lives in India and other parts of southeast Asia, where its caterpillar feeds on various shrubs.

It is related to the giant peacock moth, and also to the tussore silk moths which produce some of our

The **wild ass** from North Africa probably gave rise to the donkey.

The legs are often striped like a zebra's.

commercial silk.

ORDER: Lepidoptera
FAMILY: Saturniidae
SPECIES: *Attacus atlas*

Avadavat

A strikingly colored bird, the avadavat, or red munia, is the size of a WREN. There are three races: the Indian avadavat, the Javan avadavat, and the golden-bellied avadavat of Burma. Males are coppery to bright red with black underparts, and a reddish-brown crown. The back, rump, wings, and belly are spotted with white. The females are more somber. Avadavats preen each other.

ORDER: Passeriformes
FAMILY: Estrildidae
SPECIES: *Amandava amandava*

Avocet

Avocets are wading birds which can be identified by their long, upward-curving beaks. There are four species. Three are shore birds, while the Chilean avocet lives in the high Andes Mountains.

The Old World avocet has a distinctive and striking plumage, patterned in black and white. This pattern helps to break up the bird's body outline and thus conceal it on the ground. Such patterning is known as disruptive coloration. The American avocet and the Australian avocet have a different plumage.

Avocets live on small crustaceans, fish, mollusks, and plant material. Their curved beaks sweep the water just below the surface as they wade through the shallows. They often feed in groups, sometimes composed of as many as 300 birds.

ORDER: Charadriiformes
FAMILY: Recurvirostridae

Axis deer

Two species of axis deer live in India, the more common being the spotted deer. This is the most abundant deer in India and it is popularly known by its Hindustani name of chital. It is one of the most beautiful deer, with a bright reddish-brown coat decorated with lines of white spots and set off by conspicuous white underparts. The deer stands up to 3 ft. (90 cm) at the shoulder and lives in large herds. The males drop their slender antlers at any time of the year, and breeding also occurs at all seasons. Chital can be found throughout India and Sri Lanka, in both plains and forests. The hog deer, found on the plains between northern India and Indochina, is another axis deer, although quite unlike the chital. It is a squat, pig-like animal with short legs, and it runs rather than bounds. It does not live in large herds. Its coat is yellowish to reddish brown and slightly speckled, but the young are heavily spotted. The two species readily interbreed where their ranges meet.

ORDER: Artiodactyla
FAMILY: Cervidae
SPECIES: Spotted: *Axis axis*; hog: *Axis porcinus*

The delicately-beaked **avocet** is a wader of mud flats.

long, deep tail that helps it to swim. It breathes through feathery gills behind its head.

Axolotls live in certain lakes in Mexico. They keep to the water if possible, because their bodies might dry up on the barren land around. If the lakes dry up, axolotls become adult salamanders, able to breathe air and walk on land, but they still need to find a damp shady place to survive.

ORDER: Caudata
FAMILY: Ambystomidae
SPECIES: *Siredon mexicanum*

The face is rounded, with large eyes and naked, erect ears. Its feet and hands are unusual, especially the long, narrow middle finger of each hand, which is used for grooming, scratching, and picking the teeth as well as for probing for insects in crevices. A nocturnal animal, the aye-aye spends the day in a hollow tree or among branches. It eats insect grubs and fruit. It is named after the grating sound which it sometimes makes.

ORDER: Primates
FAMILY: Daubentonidae
SPECIES: *Daubentonia madagascariensis*

Axolotl   N, R

The axolotl is a newtlike creature with a surprising way of life. It always lives in water and lays eggs while still in its aquatic larval stage. This is as though a frog laid eggs while still a tadpole.

Axolotls are 4 to 7.2 in. (10 to 18 cm) long. They are usually black or dark brown with black spots, but albinos are quite common. The legs and feet are small and weak, but an axolotl has a

Aye-aye   E

The extremely rare aye-aye lives deep in the forests of Madagascar. When it was first found in 1780, it was thought to be a species of squirrel. Only later, when its anatomy was studied, was it seen to be a primate.

The aye-aye is the size of a cat, with a bushy tail as long as its body. The thick coat is dark brown or black, while the fur around the face is yellowish-white.

The **axolotl** is a strange amphibian that only lives in the wild in certain lakes around Mexico City.

B

Baboon   N, R

Baboons are monkeys that have forsaken a life in trees for a life on the ground, although they sleep in trees at night. Found in most parts of Africa, baboons live in close family groups, called troops. A troop may contain some old males, juveniles, females, and babies. In a small troop, there may be only one male. Their chief enemies are lions and leopards. When threatened, baboons make for the trees or rocks. When they are safe, they bark defiance and throw stones, and old males may even turn on a predator and force it to retreat. Baboons breed all year round. They eat plant and animal foods and can be serious pests when raiding crops.

Baboons are smaller than chimpanzees. They have long doglike muzzles with large teeth, and long tails. There are six species. The chacma baboon lives in eastern and southern Africa. The yellow baboon lives in central Africa. The doguera baboon ranges from Ethiopia to Kenya. The Guinea baboon is found in west-central Africa. The hamadryas, or sacred baboon, occurs in northeast Africa and Arabia. The gelada baboon is confined to Ethiopia.

ORDER: Primates
FAMILY: Cercopithecidae

Badger

Badgers are bearlike animals that belong to the same family as STOATS and WEASELS. They have stocky bodies about 1 yd. (1 m) long, short tails, and short but powerful legs armed with strong claws on the front feet. Like other members of the family, they have *musk* glands at the base of the tail and leave five-toed footprints.

The European badger is found all over Europe and Asia. It is rarely seen, however, because it is nocturnal and very wary. At a distance, the European badger's coat looks gray, but the individual hairs are actually black and white. The belly and legs of the animal are black. The most striking part of the European badger, however, is the head. This is white with two broad, black stripes running from behind the ears almost to the tip of the muzzle. The purpose of these markings is uncertain. It is un-

The European **badger** is a wary creature.

likely that they are warning colors, as badgers have no serious enemies other than human beings. It is probable, therefore, that these markings help individuals to recognize each other in the dark.

The hog badger is found in China and neighboring parts of Southeast Asia and can be distinguished from the European badger by its naked, piglike snout. The American badger is smaller than the European badger and is widespread in North America.

Badgers live in holes, or sets, excavated in the ground and filled with bracken and other vegetation for bedding. They emerge at night to feed mainly on earthworms, but also on small rodents, insects, snails, grass, nuts, and berries.

Badgers probably pair for life. Breeding begins in July or August, but the cubs are not born until the following February or March. After 6 to 8 weeks they emerge from the set, but remain with their parents for about another six months.

ORDER: Carnivora
FAMILY: Mustelidae
SPECIES: European: *Meles meles*; American: *Taxidea taxus*

Baboons spend most of their life on the ground but are still quite at home in trees.

Balance of nature

Unless disturbed by people, any one part of the country-side will always tend to support the same animals and plants. This ability of nature to remain unchanged is called the balance of nature. For example, if a stretch of grassland is able to provide food for a dozen rabbits, then a dozen rabbits will generally be found there. If too many rabbits move in, then there will not be enough food for them all. Some will either die or migrate, and the balance will be restored. Similarly, if the grassland becomes overgrown, more animals will arrive to feed on it. The same area of grassland may provide enough rabbits to feed one fox. If the fox eats all the rabbits, it too, will have to move on while the population recovers.

Over long periods there are, of course, changes. Some are cyclic, occurring every few years. For example, every four years the numbers of snowy owls in the Arctic rise to a peak level, then drop back. Over much longer periods, of thousands of years, permanent changes occur – generally due to changes of climate. For example, the lion, a warm-climate animal, was once plentiful in Europe, where the climate has now become too cold for it to survive.

Bald eagle

The bald eagle is one of the sea eagles and is famous as the national emblem of the United States. Until about seven years old, the bald eagle looks very like the golden eagle, for it has not yet developed the distinctive white feathers on the tail and head, which give the bird its popular name. Once common throughout North America, the bald eagle became rare due to hunting, loss of habitat, and the harmful effects of pesticides. Conservation programs have helped increase the bald eagle population. Bald eagles nest in trees or on cliffs, feeding on fish, rabbits, waterfowl, and even young deer.

ORDER: Falconiformes
FAMILY: Accipitridae
SPECIES: *Haliaetus leucocephalus*

The **bald eagle** is badly named. Its white head is well feathered.

Bandicoot N, R, E, Ex

Bandicoots are *marsupials* that look like rats. The 19 species of bandicoot range over parts of Australia, Tasmania, and Papua New Guinea. Bandicoots are nocturnal. Some species eat only bulbs, roots, and seeds, but others are wholly carnivorous, eating earthworms, small lizards, mice, slugs, and snails. Two species of rabbit bandicoot, sometimes called bilbies, dig burrows 3 to 6 ft. (90 to 180 cm) long in which they shelter during the hot desert days. Pig-footed bandicoots are now almost extinct. The name comes from the front feet which are cloven-hoofed, like those of a pig. But, to make this animal even stranger, the hind feet are more like those of a horse.

ORDER: Marsupialia
FAMILY: Peramelidae

Barbary ape V

The Barbary ape is the only *primate* (apart from man) which lives in Europe, in a small colony in Gibraltar. It also occurs in Algeria and Morocco. Barbary apes are monkeys of the MACAQUE family, but were called apes because they have a very small tail, which can be seen only when the animal is handled. Barbary apes are about 24 in. (60 cm) long and weigh 9 to 20 lb. (4 to 9 kg). The coat is thick, coarse and brown. They roam in large bands and are good tree climbers and balancers. Babies may be born at any time of the year.

ORDER: Primates
FAMILY: Cercopithecidae
SPECIES: *Macaca sylvanus*

The **barbary ape** is the only monkey living in Europe.

Barbary sheep V

The Barbary sheep is the only African wild sheep. It lives in dry, hilly regions in North Africa and feeds on the scattered shrubs and grasses. It stands a maximum of 3.6 ft. (109 cm) at the shoulder and weighs up to 250 lb. (115 kg). It has a short, fawn-colored coat, with a fringe of long hair that hangs down from the chest over the front legs, and a longish tail. A gland beneath the tail gives the sheep a goatlike odor. Males have smooth, thick, backward-sweeping horns. The sheep live in small herds, but the rams are often solitary, except during the mating season. Young males form bachelor herds.

ORDER: Artiodactyla
FAMILY: Bovidae
SPECIES: *Ammotragus lervia*

Barbel

The barbel is a freshwater fish of the CARP family that lives in European rivers. In the Danube, the barbel when fully grown can weigh as much as 50 lb. (23 kg). Even larger is its close relative of Indian rivers, the mahseer, an edible fish weighing up to 100 lb. (45 kg). These fish have four barbels, or feelers, around the mouth, which are studded with taste buds for the detection of small prey in the bottom mud.

ORDER: Cypriniformes
FAMILY: Cyprinidae
SPECIES: *Barbus barbus*

The **barbel** is a large river fish.

Barber fish

Barber fish is a name applied to many fish belonging to several different orders and families. These fish all have in common the habit of barbering, or cleaning, other fish, to free them from patches of dead skin and skin

Above: **Barbary sheep**, father and son; only adult males have large, backward-sweeping horns.

Below: A tiny **barber fish** (or cleaner fish) removes parasites from the mouth of a larger fish.

parasites. In this way the barber fish get their food.

Barber fish often live in a rock crevice close to a brilliantly colored sea anemone or sponge which advertises their presence. Customer fish have been observed to line up at the "sign," waiting their turn to be cleaned. A customer fish will allow the much smaller barber fish to enter its gill chambers and its mouth to make a thorough job of the cleaning. Large sharks, with their batteries of razor-sharp teeth, are often cleaned in this way without any harm coming to the little barber fish.

Bark beetle

The bark beetles are small insects related to the WEEVILS. Their larvae live just under the bark of various trees, and produce intricate patterns of tunnels as they chew their way through the nutritious tissues between the bark and the hard wood. Each species produces its own characteristic pattern, based on the original arrangement of the eggs laid under the bark by the female. Heavy infestations can reduce timber production, and the most destructive species is the elm bark beetle, which carries Dutch elm disease. This disease has killed millions of elm trees. The adult beetles, which are brown and bullet shaped, chew tender leaves and buds on the twigs.

ORDER: Coleoptera
FAMILIES: Scolytidae

When the tide is in the **barnacle** opens its bony plates and puts out feathery limbs to catch food.

Barnacle

The 800 species of barnacle are crustaceans, the adult forms of which encrust rocks, the piles of piers, and the bottoms of ships. The animal has been aptly described as "standing on its head and kicking food into its mouth." The barnacle's head is cemented firmly to rock or other underwater objects. The shell is made up of several plates, which are open while the animal is submerged, but closed if it is exposed to air by the receding tide. While submerged, the barnacle moves its feathery

Elm wood from which the bark has been removed shows the tunnels made by the **bark beetle** (inset).

legs in and out of the shell to comb food from the water.

There are two basic types of barnacle. Acorn barnacles are the most numerous animals on shore, and up to 30,000 have been found on one square yard. Most acorn barnacles are small, but one American species has a diameter of nearly 12 in. (30 cm). The second type, the goose barnacles, hang from a tough stalk that is formed from the front part of the head. The larvae of both types float freely in the sea until they settle and become adults.

ORDER: Thoracica

Barnacle goose

The barnacle goose is similar to, but smaller than, the CANADA GOOSE. Its plumage is gray with black stripes, the neck is black and

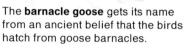

The **barnacle goose** gets its name from an ancient belief that the birds hatch from goose barnacles.

A **barn owl** flies silently. Its fluffy flight feathers muffle the noise of its wingbeats.

the head is white. It breeds in the Arctic and migrates south to parts of northern Europe for the winter. The common name dates from the Middle Ages. Before the breeding sites of barnacle geese were known, people thought that they hatched from goose barnacles because they looked something like them. They feed on a variety of plants, and on a few small animals. Unlike other geese, they build down-filled nests on the rocky ledges of cliffs.

ORDER: Anseriformes
FAMILY: Anatidae
SPECIES: *Branta leucopsis*

Barn owl

The barn owl is the most widely spread land bird in the world. Varieties are found in every continent except Antarctica. Seen flying soundlessly at dusk, the barn owl looks ghostly white. Its upperparts are actually orange-brown, speckled with gray. The underparts and heart-shaped face are pure white. Its appearance and strange shriek have made the barn owl a favorite with storytellers as a bird of ill omen. But it is in fact a most useful bird, for its prey consists largely of mice, voles, and other pests.

Barn owls often nest in old farm buildings. The female begins to incubate each egg as soon as it is laid, so the young hatch at different times. This makes the parents' task of gathering food less of a strain. Like other owls, the barn owl cannot digest fur and bones. It ejects this waste matter as pellets.

ORDER: Strigiformes
FAMILY: Tytonidae
SPECIES: *Tyto alba*

Barracuda

The barracuda is a fierce and voracious fish. It has a torpedo-shaped body, a jutting lower jaw, and a wicked set of fangs. It is a school fish when young but the largest barracudas, up to 9 ft. (2.7 m) in length, are solitary fish.

Barracudas charge through schools of prey fish with snapping bites. They may round up the rest of a school and herd it until the time comes for the barracudas' next meal. Divers often fear barracudas more than they fear SHARKS, because a barracuda hunts by sight and will attack any

Basilisks are related to the iguanas. The male has a large crest.

flashing metallic object such as a fishing spear.

ORDER: Perciformes
FAMILY: Sphyraenidae

Basilisk

There are several species of basilisks, all living in tropical America. They are iguana lizards and are named after the fabled basilisk, whose glance was said to kill. But basilisks are harmless except to the birds and rodents that they catch and eat. They also eat some vegetable food.

Basilisks grow about 2 ft. (60 cm) long. They have a long tapering tail, and males have a crest of skin that runs down the head, back, and tail. If an enemy comes near, a basilisk runs away on its long hind legs that end in long toes fringed with scales. This lizard can even run on water for a short distance without sinking.

ORDER: Squamata
FAMILY: Iguanidae
SPECIES: *Basiliscus basiliscus*

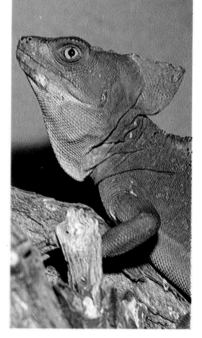

Basking shark

The basking shark is a huge but inoffensive shark, often more than 42 ft. (13 m) long. After the equally harmless whale shark, it is the largest of all sharks. These giant fish both feed on the smallest of sea creatures. They swim slowly forward with their mouths open, straining out from the seawater great quantities of the floating bodies of the tiny animals and plants of the plankton.

The basking shark lives in temperate seas throughout the world but is most common in the North Atlantic. A second species of basking shark is believed to live in seas off the coast of Australia. Basking sharks enter coastal waters in summer, either singly, or in groups and schools of up to 60 fish. They are fished chiefly for their great livers, which provide much of the world's "cod liver oil."

ORDER: Lamniformes
FAMILY: Cetorhinidae
SPECIES: *Cetorhinus maximus*

The **bass** is found chiefly along ocean coasts.

Bass

The common bass is a popular marine sport fish having the general appearance and size of a SALMON (to which, however, it is unrelated). Certain freshwater fish having spiny fins similar to those of the common bass are also known as bass. This name, then, is applied to several fish belonging to different genera, or even to different families, of fish.

The common bass and its marine relatives feed largely on PRAWNS, SHRIMP, CRABS, and small fish. One near relative, the stone bass, or wreckfish, gets the latter name from its peculiar habit of swimming close by floating wreck-

Bats' wings are supported by fingers, forelimbs, hind-limbs, and tail. This is a diagram of a pipistrelle.

Tail membrane

Shin

Finger-tips

3rd   4th   5th

Greater mouse-eared bat

2nd finger

Thumb   Forearm

Noctule

Common long-eared bat

Natterer's bat

Whiskered bat

age. Many other relatives of the common bass are *hermaphrodite*, with both male and female sex organs, while others are *inter-sexes*, changing from male to female or vice versa.

ORDER: Perciformes
FAMILY: Serranidae

Bat   N, R, V, E, Ex

Of all the world's mammals, bats are the only ones that can really fly. Most of the 18 families and 180 genera of bats live in the tropics, but they are widely distributed throughout warm and temperate climates in both hemispheres.

They do not inhabit polar or high mountain regions.

Bats are acrobatic fliers. Their wings are extensions of the skin of their bellies and back. The skin is stretched between the "fingers" of the forelimbs, the sides of the body, and the hind limbs. Their flying action has been likened to swimming in air. The animal operates its wings by coordinated movements of arms and legs similar to a swimmer doing the breast stroke. Many species have a further membrane joining the hind legs. The tail is generally completely enclosed in this membrane.

Like other mammals, bats

suckle their young. They are warm-blooded and furry. Females usually bear only one offspring each season. Hibernating species of bats generally mate in the autumn. The male's sperm is held in the female's reproductive tract until winter is past. Then she releases the sperm to fertilize her *ovum* in spring. This delay in the fertilization of the egg ensures that birth will occur at a suitable season. The young bats of some species stay with their mothers even in flight, clinging to the mother's fur with their milk teeth. Although slow to breed, bats keep up their numbers because they live a long time; more than 20 years in the wild.

Many bats that live in temperate regions hibernate in cold weather. They hang upside down, hooking their feet into a crevice in the roof of a cave or in a hollow tree. Their body heat falls, and all body processes slow down. Their intake of oxygen drops to one-hundredth of its normal level. Even when sleeping during the day at an active time of year, bats may become torpid, but quickly recover normal temperature when they wake for the night's food gathering.

Contrary to what many people think, bats see quite well, but most species find their food at night when they must use means other than sight. They have a good sense of smell, but depend principally on echolocation. They utter high-pitched sounds extremely rapidly, between 100 and 200 times a second. These sound waves hit objects in the bats' flight path and are echoed back to the bats' ears. The echoes of these pulsing cries tell a bat what is in its path even in total darkness. If it is pursuing an insect, a bat locates it by echo, then makes a "lap" of its wings to guide the creature into its jaws. Bats eat a wide variety of foods. These include insects, fish, blood, fruit, and nectar.

Bat species vary greatly in size. The smallest is the bumblebee bat

The fruit-eating **bat** has a face that strongly resembles that of a fox. It is often called a flying fox.

which is just over 1 in. (2.5 cm) long with a wingspan of about 6 in. (15 cm). The largest is one of the FLYING FOX, with a wingspan of about 6 ft. (1.8 m) and body length of 16 in. (40 cm).

ORDER: Chiroptera

The **grizzly bear** is at home in water. This one is probably hunting for salmon or trout.

Bat-eared fox

The bat-eared, or big-eared fox, has a narrow face, long ears, a limp brush, and a yellowish coat. It resembles a JACKAL. With a length of 18 to 23 in. (46 to 58 cm) it is much the same size as a RED FOX, but at 6.6 to 10 lb. (3 to 4.5 kg), it is barely half the weight.

Bat-eared foxes are found in open sandy ground in most parts of Africa, where their main enemies are man and leopards. They are nocturnal, but the animals' strong curiosity brings them out in daylight, usually in pairs. Their diet consists mainly of termites and other insects which they crush with their pointed teeth. But they will also eat small rodents, carrion, nestlings, and eggs. The animal's hearing is very sensitive. Their young are born in litters of two to five, usually in the rainy season.

ORDER: Carnivora
FAMILY: Canidae
SPECIES: *Octocyon megalotis*

Bear

Bears are large mammals with powerful limbs, strong claws, and short tails. Like BADGERS, they differ from other carnivores in that they eat plants as well as flesh. They are mainly slow-moving

ground dwellers but they can walk on their hind legs and climb trees.

The northern members of the family are the American BLACK BEAR, the BROWN BEAR, and the POLAR BEAR. Other species include the moon bear, or Himalayan black bear, the SLOTH BEAR, or Indian bear, the Malayan SUN BEAR, and the SPECTACLED BEAR of South America.

ORDER: Carnivora
FAMILY: Ursidae

The **beaver** fells a tree by cutting chips from the trunk with its large front teeth. It is a skilled dam and lodge builder (right).

Beaver   N, E

There are two species of beaver. The European beaver is now found only in Scandinavia, along rivers in European Russia, and in the Elbe and Rhone valleys. The endangered North American beaver has been reduced in numbers by fur trapping and the loss of its habitat. It survives in Canada and the northern United States.

Among the rodents, only the CAPYBARA is larger than the beaver. Stout-bodied with dark brown fur, the beaver is about 1 yd. (1 m) long, with a broad flat tail, powerful limbs, and a blunt muzzle. It has five toes on each foot. Those on the front feet are strongly clawed, and are used for digging, handling food, and carrying sticks and mud. The hind feet are webbed for swimming, with special split claws which the beaver uses for grooming its dense fur and heavy outer coat, and for spreading oil to act as a water-proofing insulation. The tail is used as a rudder when the beaver is swimming, and as a support when the animal stands up on dry land to gnaw at trees. Underwater, the beaver's nostrils and ears close automatically, and it can stay submerged for up to 15 minutes.

Beavers, probably the best-known of nature's "engineers," live in small family groups. They are skilled at felling trees and building dams in order to provide themselves with a safe home and a guaranteed food supply. Their home may be a burrow in a bank

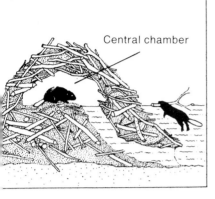

Central chamber

or a "lodge" in a pond made by damming a river. To fell trees, the beaver uses its large cutting *incisor* teeth as chisels to chew chips out of the trunks. It feeds on bark and sapwood, using larger branches as building material for the dam and lodge. The upper half of the lodge projects above water; inside is a dry central chamber, with one or more escape tunnels leading to underwater exits.

Beavers have been hunted for their fur and for their *musk*. Their natural enemies include the WOLVERINE, COYOTE, WOLF, LYNX, PUMA, and BEAR. When alarmed, the beaver warns of danger by smacking its broad tail onto the water.

ORDER: Rodentia
FAMILY: Castoridae
SPECIES: North American: *Castor canadiensis*; European: *Castor fiber*

Bee

The bees belong to the same group of insects as the WASP and ANTS. They all have four wings, but the hind ones are small and linked to the front wings by rows of tiny hooks. The insects are mostly brown or black and, unlike wasps, they are generally quite furry. The female nearly always carries a stinger, although there are some stingerless species. The stinger is used for defense. Bees have both sucking and biting mouthparts and they feed on nectar and pollen which they collect from the

A queen **bee** lays one egg in each of the cells made by the workers. The workers surround the queen to clean and feed her.

flowers. They play a vital role in the pollination of many plants, including many important fruit crops. Nectar is collected with the tongue, while pollen is picked up on the body hairs. Much of the food is taken back to the nest to be stored or fed to the grubs, although the nectar is converted to honey before it is stored.

The HONEYBEE and the BUMBLE-BEE, together with a few other kinds of bees, are social insects. They live in colonies of anything from a few dozen to several thousand individuals. All the members work for the good of the colony as a whole. Most bees, however, are solitary insects and, after mating, each female provides

just for herself and her own offspring. Each female excavates a small nest burrow in the ground or in dead wood, or even in loose mortar in buildings, and stocks it with pollen and nectar. Eggs are laid, usually one to each chamber of the nest, and the female then closes up the entrance and flies away. She does not normally have any further contact with her eggs or grubs, which feed happily on the stored food and emerge as adults a few months later. There are a few species, however, in which the female stays around her nest and brings further food supplies as the grubs get bigger.

Cuckoo bees, as their name suggests, do not make their own nests. Some lay their eggs in bumblebee nests and rely on the bumblebees to feed the grubs. Others lay their eggs in the nests of

solitary bees, and their grubs live off the food stored for the rightful occupants. The cuckoo bees do not possess pollen baskets or other equipment for gathering and collecting pollen because they never need to stock any nests.
ORDER: Hymenoptera
FAMILY: Apidae

Bee-eater

Bee-eaters make up a family of brilliantly colored birds. They vary in length from 6 to 14 in. (15 to 36 cm), and are related to KING-FISHERS and ROLLERS, which are also noted for their bright colors. They live in tropical regions of Asia and Africa, although a few species extend into milder temperate areas. Bee-eaters nest in burrows dug with the bill and feet in sandy banks, though in Africa they sometimes use the burrows of AARDVARKS. They get their name from their habit of catching bees and wasps, which they can do without being stung. They also eat dragonflies, beetles, and flies, seizing the insects in flight.
ORDER: Coraciiformes
FAMILY: Meropidae

A **carmine bee-eater**, one of the most colorful of all African birds.

Beetle

The beetles form the largest of the insect orders, with more than 350,000 known species. They include the bulkiest of all insects – the fist-sized Goliath beetles, which may weigh about 3.5 oz. (100 g) – and also some of the smallest, with lengths of less than .02 in. (.5 mm). There are normally two pairs of wings, but the front ones are hard and horny and conceal the delicate hind wings for most of the time. The front wings are called *elytra*, and they meet in a straight line down the middle of the insect's back. In most beetles, they cover the whole of the abdomen, but some groups, notably the ROVE BEETLES, have very short elytra and a naked abdomen. Some beetles have no hind wings, and some, such as the female GLOWWORM, have no wings at all.

Beetles live just about everywhere on earth. Many live in fresh water, usually carrying their air supplies around with them under their elytra. All beetles have biting jaws and can eat most kinds of solid food. Some also manage to lap up nectar and other liquid foods. LADYBUGS, GROUND BEETLES, and the fast-running tiger beetles are predatory creatures, feeding largely on other insects.

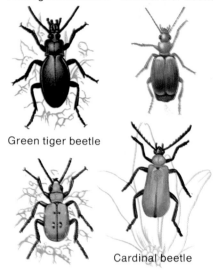

Violet ground beetle   Bombardier beetle

Green tiger beetle

Cardinal beetle

Four types of the vast group of **beetles**: the **violet ground beetle** is flightless; the **bombardier beetle** can fire a jet of corrosive liquid when disturbed.

Glowworms and many other terrestrial species are also predators, and so are most of the WATER BEETLES. The latter often attack fish and other creatures much larger than themselves. Thousands of beetles are vegetarians, feeding on all parts of plants including hard, dry seeds, and the wood of tree

The **oil beetle** can discharge an oily liquid when alarmed.

trunks. Many of these plant-eating species are serious pests, causing huge losses of grain and other foodstuffs in the fields and also in warehouses. Wood-boring beetles, such as the DEATHWATCH BEETLE and the FURNITURE BEETLE, cause severe damage to buildings and to furniture. There are also hordes of scavenging beetles, which feed on dung and carrion or make a living from the debris that accumulates in the nests of birds and other animals. Several of these debris-feeding species find their way into houses, where they feed on carpets and other fabrics.

Beetle larvae vary even more in form than the adults, although they usually inhabit the same places and feed on similar foods. They also have biting jaws like those of the adults. Ground beetle larvae are active runners with strong legs on which to chase their prey, but the larvae of most leaf-feeding beetles are sluggish creatures with soft, fat bodies and short legs. DUNG BEETLE larvae and those living in timber are surrounded by food and do not have to move much. They generally have fat bodies, often curved in a C-shape, and short legs. WEEVIL larvae, which are also usually surrounded by food, have no legs at all.

All beetles pass through a *pupa* stage between the larval and adult stages. Adults can be found at all times of year, even in cold climates. Some fly readily, but others are reluctant to fly, even when disturbed, and the wingless ones, of course, are unable to fly.
ORDER: Coleoptera

Bellbird

The name given to several species of unrelated birds whose song has a metallic ring. There are four species related to the COTINGAS, which live in the forests of South and Central America. One of these, the three-wattled bellbird, has an odd appearance with its three gray-black, turkeylike

A **bighorn** ewe is feeding on sparse winter grass.

wattles dangling from the base of its bill. The crested bellbird of Australia is a colorful bird, reddish-brown above and white below. It is related to the FLY-CATCHERS and feeds on grubs, insects, and seeds.
ORDER: Passeriformes

Beluga

The beluga, or white whale, is a relative of the DOLPHIN. It grows to about 20 ft. (6 m) in length, and lives in Arctic waters, often swimming up rivers.

Under water the beluga "talks" in a series of whistles, earning it the whalers' nickname of "sea canary." One of the toothed whales, the beluga feeds on fish, shrimp, cuttlefish, and crabs.

Belugas were once seen in enormous schools of as many as 10,000 individuals, but whaling has greatly reduced their numbers. Normally they move in groups of about a dozen. Their chief enemy is the killer whale.
ORDER: Cetacea
FAMILY: Monodontidae
SPECIES: *Delphinapterus leucas*

Bichir

The bichir is a fish of the Nile River, with many extraordinary and primitive features. Like other fish it has gills, but it uses its *swim bladder* to breathe air, and if held under water it will drown. Also, the bichir's swim bladder is paired like the lungs of a land animal, whereas in most other fish it is single.

The bichir has been described as a missing link between the two great groups of fish – the cartilaginous fishes, or sharks, and the bony, or true, fish.

The bichir has peculiar front fins, shaped like legs, on which it stalks its prey on the riverbed, rather as a cat stalks a mouse. It finds its prey in the mud with the aid of tube-shaped nostrils, yet another strange feature of this most unusual fish.
ORDER: Polypteriformes
FAMILY: Polypteridae
SPECIES: *Polypterus bichir*

Bighorn

The bighorn is a wild sheep which lives in western North America in dry upland country or above the tree line. Males have huge horns that curve around the back of the head. In old animals, the horns come forward to the level of the eyes. Females have small, slightly curving horns. These powerful animals have little to fear except man. Mating occurs in winter and the young are born six and a half months later. Bighorn sheep, both male and female, sometimes charge at each other and crash head on. Such bone-jarring combats may last for hours.

ORDER: Artiodactyla
FAMILY: Bovidae
SPECIES: *Ovis canadensis*

Bird-eating spider

The bird-eating spiders are among the largest living SPIDERS, having a leg span of up to 8 in. (20 cm). They live in the Amazon forests of South America, where they hunt small mammals and drag hummingbirds from their nests. They do not spin a web. These spiders are not particularly dangerous to humans; the venom is about as painful as a bee sting, but the body is covered with fine hairs which can irritate the skin of anyone who handles it. The bird-eating spiders are sometimes referred to as tarantulas, but the true TARANTULA is a wolf spider found in southern Europe.

ORDER: Araneae
FAMILY: Aviculariidae

A **bird-eating spider** has seized a locust and plunged in its great fangs.

The great **bird of paradise** are beautiful birds confined to New Guinea and Australia.

Bird of paradise   N, R, V

The name given to the 43 species of the most colorful and ornate bird family. All live in the forests of New Guinea and neighboring small islands, apart from four species which live in the mountain forests of northeast Australia. Most birds of paradise have long, lacy plumes extending well beyond the tail when they are at rest. When displaying, the plumes form a fan over the back. Courtship displays are often long, elaborate, and acrobatic. Some species have rather dull plumage, and the males and females are alike, but in the majority, the sexes differ markedly. The females are dull but the males have brightly colored plumage. The numbers of many species were severely reduced by local use of the feathers in headdresses and by their export overseas for the fashion industry. Restrictions imposed in the 1920s have helped some species to recover.

ORDER: Passeriformes
FAMILY: Paradisaeidae

Birdwing butterfly N, V, E

The birdwings include some of the largest and most beautiful of all butterflies. They live in the forests of Southeast Asia and New Guinea, and some of the females exceed 10 in. (25 cm) in wingspan. The males are a little smaller, but much more colorful, with velvety black wings marked with beautiful iridescent colors. Males sometimes congregate in their hundreds to drink from muddy riverbanks.

ORDER: Lepidoptera
FAMILY: Papilionidae

Bishop bird

Bishop birds make up a group of birds within the family of WEAVER-BIRDS, which also includes the SPARROWS. They are small birds, about 5 in. (13 cm) long, and are found in tropical and subtropical regions of Africa, often in open grassland or clearings in forests. Outside the breeding season, bishop birds are dull colored, like sparrows, but at breeding time, the males don bright colors; the fire-crowned bishop bird becomes bright red and black for example.

Birds

Birds belong to the animal class Aves and are distinguished from all other animals by their feathers. The front limbs have been turned into wings, although not all birds can actually fly. Birds are warm-blooded, which means that they can keep their bodies at a constant high temperature regardless of the surrounding temperatures, and thus work more efficiently.

Modern birds have no teeth, but their horny beaks serve the same purpose. The beaks vary in shape according to the diet. All bird species lay eggs, and there is often a long period of parental care before the young birds are able to fend for themselves.

There are 27 orders of living birds. Just over 5,000 of the 8,600 species belong to just one order – the Passeriformes, or perching birds. These are also known as songbirds, and they include all the small birds of the forest and countryside as well as a few larger ones such as the CROWS.

A **great tit** in flight.

The embryo grows inside the egg until it is ready to hatch. It breathes air from the space at the end, and gets its food from the yolk.

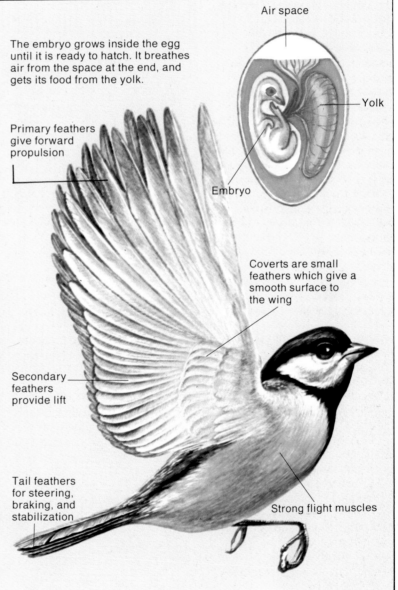

Air space

Yolk

Embryo

Primary feathers give forward propulsion

Coverts are small feathers which give a smooth surface to the wing

Secondary feathers provide lift

Tail feathers for steering, braking, and stabilization

Strong flight muscles

Bishop birds are renowned for their polygamy, which is unusual among birds, each male mating with up to six females.
ORDER: Passeriformes
FAMILY: Ploceidae

Bison N, V

There are two species of bison: the American bison, often incorrectly called the buffalo; and the European bison or wisent. These massive, oxlike animals weigh up to 3,000 lb. (1,360 kg). The largest stand 6 ft. (183 cm) at the shoulder, which is raised in a hump. The hair on the head, neck, shoulders, and forelegs is long and shaggy. The forehead is broad and both sexes have two short, curving horns. The American bison has a longer coat than the wisent, the horns are smaller and less curved, and the hindquarters are smaller. There are two varieties of American bison. The plains bison is smaller and lighter in color than the wood bison of Canada, but it has a heavier head and hump.

Bison live in herds, which once numbered thousands of animals. North America once had 50 million bison but by 1889 only 540 were left. The American Indians killed bison for food, but it was the Europeans who massacred the herds. They killed bison for their meat and skins and also for sport. European bison also nearly became extinct, as their forest habitat was destroyed. The last truly wild bison, in the Bialowieza forest of Poland, were killed during World War I. But European bison were bred in zoos and, in 1959, a herd was reestablished in Bialowieza. The American plains bison now number several thousands and Canadian wood bison are protected in a reserve in Alberta. Bison mate between July and September, and gestation takes about nine months.
ORDER: Artiodactyla
FAMILY: Bovidae
SPECIES: American: *Bison bison*; European: *Bison bonasus*

The male red **bishop bird**.

Bitterling

This small, freshwater fish of European rivers is notable for its remarkable breeding behavior. This involves a freshwater mussel, which is both the breeding ground of the fish and also a kind of partner.

During the breeding season the female bitterling develops a long tube through which she lays her eggs in the gills of the mussel. The male bitterling then exudes his milt, or sperm, also into the

The **bitterling** is about 3.6 in. (9 cm) long.

mussel, but through its *siphon*. Fertilization of the eggs and early development of the fish take place entirely inside the mussel, with the little fish, or *fry*, only leaving after about a month. But at the time of egg laying, the mussel also produces its larvae, which attach themselves to the female bitterling's skin. There they feed and develop for three months, before dropping from the fish as small but perfectly formed mussels.
ORDER: Cypriniformes
FAMILY: Cyprinidae
SPECIES: *Rhodeus sericeus*

Bittern

Bitterns are a subfamily of the HERONS. Like herons, bitterns have long, pointed bills but the neck is shorter and thicker than that of the common heron and the body is rather smaller. The plumage is brown, mottled with black, with a white chin and black cap. The feathers down the front of the neck are long, forming a kind of ruff. The most familiar species in Europe is known for its booming call, like the bellow of a bull. The American bittern differs from the European species in that it has a black patch on either side of the neck, the plumage is more streaked, and it does not have a black cap. Bitterns feed on animals living in reed beds, where they also nest.
ORDER: Ciconiiformes
FAMILY: Ardeidae

Bird with a booming call – the **bittern**.

Black bear N, V

There are five species of black bear, all of them smaller than the BROWN BEAR. The best-known species is the American Black bear, which is up to 5 ft. (1.5 m) long and weighs up to 500 lb. (230 kg). The fur is not always black; it may be chocolate brown, cinnamon brown, or blue-black. However, the black bear can be distinguished from the brown bear by its shorter fur and claws. The Himalayan black bear is similar to the American but is distinguished by a pale V-shaped mark on its chest.

Black bears originally roamed in all the wooded areas of North America. They have since been eliminated from much of their former range, but are increasing in national parks where they have become used to humans and are harmless unless provoked or allowed to become overfriendly.

Black bears breed in June and gestation takes 100 to 210 days. However, black bears sleep through the winter (but do not hibernate in the true sense) and when the cubs are born in January, the mother only rouses herself sufficiently to bite through the *umbilical cords* before continuing her sleep for another two months. Meanwhile, the cubs, blind and weighing only 10 ounces (280 g) at birth, alternately drink her milk and sleep. They remain with their mother for six months.

The black bear is the original "teddy bear." In 1902 Theodore (Teddy) Roosevelt, then President of the United States, caught a black bear and took it home as a pet. Morris Michton, a New York toymaker, then had the idea of manufacturing the small fur-covered teddy bears that have since become so popular all over the world.

ORDER: Carnivora
FAMILY: Ursidae

Blackbird N, V

The European blackbird is a member of the THRUSH family, with races in Asia and North Africa. A bird of hedgerows and thickets, it is also common in

Male

Female

The male European **blackbird** is all black, with a bright yellow beak. The female is dark brown all over and is sometimes confused with the thrush. Some blackbirds are albinos that have white patches, or may even be entirely white.

Below: A male **blackbird** brings a beakful of insects for its ravenous brood.

gardens and on farms. The male is 10 in. (25 cm) long, has a yellow bill and a glossy black plumage. The female is more brown, with a brown bill and a speckled breast, and is sometimes confused with a thrush. The blackbird has a rich song, but it is perhaps best known for its rattlelike alarm note which also serves as a warning to other birds that a predator is around. Blackbirds feed especially on berries and soft fruits, but also eat worms, grubs, seeds, and snails.

The New World blackbirds belong to an entirely different family from the European species. The red-winged blackbird is found throughout most of North America, and is so named for the red and yellow tipped shoulders of the male. They live in swamps and marshes, nesting among the reeds. Their diet consists mostly of insects and seed. The yellow-headed blackbird lives in the western U.S. and southern Canada.

ORDER: Passeriformes
FAMILIES: Turdidae (European); Icteridae (New World)

Blackbuck

The blackbuck, or Indian antelope, is one of the fastest land animals, being credited with speeds of 50 mph (80 km/h) when alarmed. It can leap about 6 ft. (1.8 m) into the air and can cover up to 24 ft. (7 m) in one bound. The blackbuck is found on the open plains of Pakistan and southern and central India, where it lives in herds ruled by a dominant male. It is just under 4 ft. (122 cm) long and weighs up to 80 lb. (36 kg). The adult male is a different color from the female. The upperparts of the buck are a dark brown, while those of the doe and the young are yellowish-fawn. Only the buck has horns.

ORDER: Artiodactyla
FAMILY: Bovidae
SPECIES: *Antilope cervicapra*

Black-headed gull

The black-headed gull is one of the smaller gulls. It is distinguished from other gulls by the chocolate-brown "hood" on its head. In winter, the hood disappears, except for small patches on the sides of the head and in front of the eyes. The body is white, with a gray back and wings. The wing tips are black and the bill and legs red. Black-headed gulls are found over most of Europe and Asia, not only around shores but also inland, where they may follow plows or search for scraps in towns.

ORDER: Charadriiformes
FAMILY: Laridae
SPECIES: *Larus ridibundus*

Black widow spider

This species of spider is found all over the warmer parts of the world. The North American species is feared for its powerful venom, but although its attack is painful it is rarely fatal unless its victims are very young, old, or unwell. The venom seems to be strongest in the subspecies which lives in the southern United States. The black widow spins an irregular web, which often includes a short funnel of silk; the male's web is smaller. The spider inhabits cool, dark places, such as cellars and outbuildings. It appears that most human victims are attacked in primitive latrines. Death, when it does result, is probably caused by shock.

People believe that the black widow gets her name because she eats her mate. Although this is sometimes the case, males in captivity have been known to mate with several females.

ORDER: Araneae
FAMILY: Theridiidae
SPECIES: *Latrodectus mactans*

Blenny

The common name of a very large assemblage of fish belonging to 20 or so different families. Mostly, these fish are small inhabitants of shallow areas of temperate and

An African **black widow spider** spinning its web; the red spot may have an hourglass shape.

tropical seas. Many live near the shoreline and can often be found lurking under stones or in seaweed. They are also commonly found in rock pools after the retreat of the tide.

A common feature of these species of fish is a long *dorsal fin* that extends from the back of the head along the back, either nearly reaching the tail or completely fusing with it. Most blennies seem to eat a wide variety of foods. In their inshore waters, they are easy prey for sharp-eyed gulls or scavenging rats, but they get some protection from camouflage. They are able to change the mottled patterns of their bodies to match their stony background.

ORDER: Perciformes
FAMILY: Blenniidae and others

Blister beetle

The many species of blister beetles are soft-bodied insects with soft *elytra*. They get their name because they contain a substance

Male Montagu's **blennies** are blue spotted.

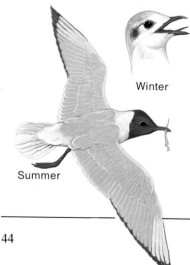

Winter

Summer

called cantharidin, which causes blistering of the skin. Merely touching one of these insects, especially on the elytra, can cause a burning sensation and painful blisters. Most species possess bright warning colors. They live mainly in dry climates, but the Spanish fly, a handsome metallic green insect, is widespread in the southern half of Europe. The adult feeds on various trees and shrubs, but the larva lives as a parasite in the nests of solitary bees. Most other blister beetle grubs live in this way, although some attack grasshopper eggs.

ORDER: Coleoptera
FAMILY: Meloidae

Blowfly

This name is given to several species of stout flies whose maggots develop in rotting flesh. Best known are the bluebottles and greenbottles which are beautifully colored with metallic sheens, but have unpleasant habits. Bluebottles regularly enter houses in their search for meat or fish in which to lay their eggs, and their noisy flight can be most annoying. Greenbottles are less inclined to come inside, but can often be seen resting on sunny walls. They lay their eggs in various sorts of carrion, and often on living ani-

Right: The **greenbottle** and **bluebottle** with maggot; Below: A greenbottle sucking up its food.

mals, especially sheep. The resulting maggots feed on the living flesh, causing serious sores.

ORDER: Diptera
FAMILY: Calliphoridae

Bluefish

The bluefish is a fast-swimming and fierce ocean fish, about 16 in. (40 cm) long, with a bluish or greenish body. It lives in large schools. Bluefish schools roam tropical and subtropical waters, and the trail of such a school is often marked by widespread blood and fragments of fish, showing the damage it has inflicted on other schools of fish. Bluefish occur in quite incredible numbers. The population of the western Atlantic in summer has been estimated at one thousand million. Moreover, each bluefish is likely to kill 10 other fish each day! 39 million lb. (18 million kg) of bluefish are caught each year for food.

ORDER: Perciformes
FAMILY: Pomatomidae
SPECIES: *Pomatomus saltatrix*

Blue butterfly   N, V, E, Ex

The blue butterflies, of which there are several hundred species, are small insects related to the COPPER and HAIRSTREAK butterflies. They get their name because the males of most of the species are bright blue on the upper side. The females are usually brown, with a greater or lesser scattering of blue

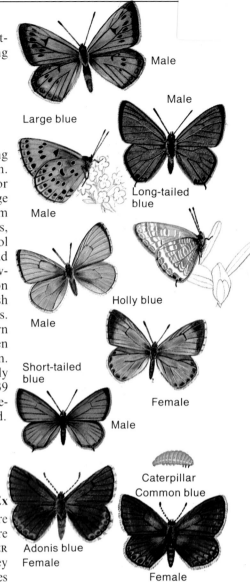

Male
Large blue
Male
Male
Long-tailed blue
Male
Holly blue
Male
Short-tailed blue
Female
Male
Adonis blue Female
Caterpillar
Common blue
Female

Below: The male **common blue**, one of the most common butterflies.

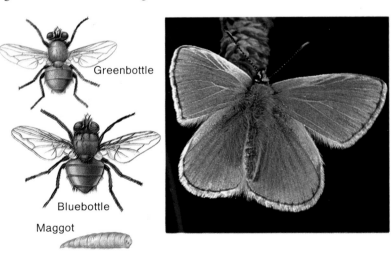

Greenbottle
Bluebottle
Maggot

scales around the wing bases. The undersides of both sexes are usually decorated with black and white eye spots and often bear orange spots around the margins. The hind wings often carry small "tails," but in some tropical species, popularly known as "back-to-front" butterflies, these projections are very long and look like additional antennae. Black spots at the hind margin of the wing resemble eyes, and the whole effect is to produce a false head at the hind end when the butterfly is at rest. This arrangement deceives many birds, which attack the hind end instead of the true head. The butterfly can then fly away, for it is not harmed if small parts of its wings are torn. Most blues of the temperate regions inhabit grasslands, where their larvae feed on vetches and related plants. The caterpillars of the North American harvester and its Asian relatives prey on aphids. The European large blue has a truly amazing life history, during which the caterpillars are collected by ants and taken into their nest. The caterpillars are fed with young ants, and in return they give out a sugary substance which the ants lap up eagerly. Many tropical blues live in the forests.

ORDER: Lepidoptera
FAMILY: Lycaenidae

Blue whale   V

The blue whale is the largest animal that has ever lived. It can reach a length of 100 ft. (30 m) and a weight of 135 tons. Sadly, its great size has made it a target for

The largest **blue whale** ever caught was over 108 ft. (33 m) in length.

the whaler's harpoon. Over-hunting in the Arctic and Antarctic Oceans, by whaling fleets eager for the vast quantities of blubber in the blue whale, has so reduced its numbers that the species is now on the brink of extinction.

Blue whales are baleen whales (see WHALE). They swallow enormous amounts of food to supply energy to their huge bodies, and a blue whale's stomach has been found to contain two tons of krill. They usually swim alone or in small groups. Apart from man, their only enemy is the killer whale, which will attack young blue whales. When danger threatens, other whales will come to the aid of their fellow, and a male never deserts a harpooned female – thereby sealing his own fate.

ORDER: Cetacea
FAMILY: Balaenopteridae
SPECIES: *Balaenoptera musculus*

Boa

Boas are part of the Boidae family, which also includes PYTHONS. The most well-known species, but by no means the largest, is the boa constrictor. Averaging 9 to 12 ft. (3 to 4 m) and weighing around 130 lb. (60 kg), this ground-dwelling snake lives among forest flora in the warmest parts of the Americas, from Mexico to northern Argentina.

As its name suggests, the boa constrictor kills its prey by squeezing or constricting. Death is by suffocation rather than crushing – the victim's ribcage is squeezed so tightly it cannot fill its lungs. Large lizards, birds, and small mammals are common prey, but tales of boas constricting human

victims to death are farfetched. In fact, boa constrictors have been kept as pets on Brazilian farms, to control rats and mice.

Other boas include the ANACONDA, the largest reptile in the world, and less well-known species like the sand boas and tree boas. Most boas prefer habitats with an abundance of plant life and water, but sand boas have adapted to life in dry regions. Living just beneath the surface, their bodies can withstand extremes of heat. Tree boas have also adapted their bodies to fit their surroundings. Beautiful green coloration and flattened bodies, which allow them to press close to tree branches, are ideal camouflage for forest life.

ORDER: Squamata
FAMILY: Boidae
SPECIES: *Constrictor constrictor* (boa constrictor)

Bobcat

The bobcat is the North American equivalent of the European WILDCAT. Bobcats weigh up to 20 lb. (9 kg) and measure up to 3 ft. (90 cm) including the very short tail. The ears are tipped with pointed tufts, rather like those of the closely related LYNX. Experiments suggest that the tufts somehow help the ears collect sounds. Most bobcats are brown, spotted with gray, or white. Their range stretches from Canada to Mexico, including habitats from deserts to forests.

These solitary creatures hunt at night. The size of each animal's range may be 5 to 50 miles (8 to 80 km) across according to the food supply the range holds. Bobcats mainly hunt rabbits and rodents, but will tackle many other kinds of prey, even killing deer and domestic livestock. Most females give birth to two kits, usually at the end of winter. The young are prey to foxes and horned owls. Adult bobcats are killed by PUMAS and they are widely persecuted by man.

ORDER: Carnivora
FAMILY: Felidae
SPECIES: *Lynx rufus*

Bollworm

This name is given to the caterpillars of several kinds of moths that feed in the seed capsules, or bolls, of cotton. The most serious of these pests is the cotton bollworm which also attacks corn and many other crops. The adult moth is pale brown and about 1.4 in (3.5 cm) across the wings. The female lays her eggs on the leaves and flowers, and the caterpillars nibble any part of the plant at first. They eventually make their way into the bolls and eat the seeds, so that the cotton fibers fail to develop.

ORDER: Lepidoptera
FAMILY: Noctuidae

Bonito

This is the name given to a number of large relatives of MACKERELS. All are important edible fish, living mainly in tropical and subtropical parts of the Atlantic and more sparingly in temperate parts of this ocean. These lively, streamlined fish are also caught for sport.

Bonito are hunting fish, swimming in schools when young but becoming more solitary with age. Sailors on sailing ships knew the large bonito well because they were likely to appear whenever the ship had flushed a school of flying fish, which are the bonito's favorite food. Bonito are not among the fastest swimmers of the mackerel family, their fastest recorded swimming speed being a mere 10 mph (16 km/h), far less than that of their great relatives the tuna.

ORDER: Perciformes
FAMILY: Scombridae

Bontebok   R, V

The bontebok was nearly wiped out by hunters in the 1800s. It was saved by a farmer in Cape Province, South Africa, who enclosed some of these fast-running antelopes on his land and established a breeding herd. Today, bontebok can be seen only on private farms and in national parks. The bontebok stands about 4 ft. (122 cm) at the shoulder and weighs up to 200 lb. (90 kg). The horns are 15 to 16 in. (38 to 41 cm) long. The name bontebok means "painted buck," and this glossy reddish-brown animal has a white blaze on the face, a white rump and, white on the insides of the legs.

ORDER: Artiodactyla
FAMILY: Bovidae
SPECIES: *Damaliscus pygargus*

Booby   N, E

Six species of the GANNET family which live in tropical regions are known as boobies. The name

A pair of **boobies** perform the first steps of their ritual courtship dance which will end with the female touching the male's bill or neck. The female builds a cup-shaped nest.

comes from the Spanish word "bobo," meaning "dunce." Boobies are so called because they are clumsy on land and do not fear human beings. They are goose-sized birds, with thick necks and large heads, and long, powerful wings.

All boobies nest in colonies, with the birds usually crowded together, but nesting sites vary. Pairs are slow to form, but once formed, a pair stays together for life. The nest is built of seaweed, feathers, fish bones, and droppings which the male collects and deposits in front of the female as she builds up a cup-shaped nest. Two eggs are laid but rarely more than one is reared.

ORDER: Pelecaniformes
FAMILY: Sulidae

Book louse

Book lice, also called dust lice, are very small, flattened, wingless insects that are usually found indoors in dusty corners and among piles of books and papers. They feed on debris and on the tiny molds associated with it. There are numerous species, and they belong to a group called psocids. This group also includes many winged insects that live on tree trunks. These are called bark lice because they chew the algae on the bark.
ORDER: Psocoptera

Boomslang

The boomslang is one of the few rearfanged snakes which are dangerous to man. Boomslang bites are usually fatal, unless very quickly treated. The venom runs down grooves in some of the teeth in the back part of the upper jaw. This slender, bright green snake lives in Africa. It slides gracefully among branches well above the ground where it hunts for birds, tree lizards, and small mammals. It often snatches eggs and fledglings from their nests. The female lays her eggs in a warm, moist hollow, often in a sandy bank, but sometimes in a woodpecker's nest hole in a tree.
ORDER: Squamata
FAMILY: Colubridae
SPECIES: *Dispholidus typus*

A male **satin bowerbird** sits in the bower of twigs it has built.

Bowerbird N, R

The name given to a number of species of birds that build "bowers" from twigs, grass, leaves, and other plant material. The bower is used by the male bowerbird as a center point for the elaborate courtship displays with which he attracts a mate. After mating, the female builds a simple nest away from the bower.

Bowerbirds live in Australia and New Guinea. The bower may vary in complexity from a simple clearing on the ground to a tall tower with a tepeelike roof. Some have many compartments. They are nearly always decorated with brightly colored and glittering objects – snail shells, seeds, pebbles, dead insects and feathers, for example. Manmade objects are also used, such as bottle tops. Three species actually mix pigments and paint the walls of their bowers.

ORDER: Passeriformes
FAMILY: Ptilonorhynchidae

Bowfin

The bowfin is a primitive fish that lives in lakes and rivers of North America. It is like a PIKE in shape and size, with powerful jaws that show it is a predator. Like LUNG-FISH, the bowfin lives in sluggish

The **brambling** can be recognized by its orange breast.

Female

Male
(summer)

Male
(winter)

waters containing little dissolved oxygen, and, like them, it uses its *swim bladder* to breathe air. The male fish makes a nest and guards the eggs and young.

ORDER: Amiiformes
FAMILY: Amiidae
SPECIES: *Amia calva*

Brambling

The brambling looks like a CHAF-FINCH, but differs in having a white rump and less white on the wings. It also has a bold orange shoulder patch and breast, and the male has a black (not blue) head and mantle in spring and summer. This attractive bird breeds in the far north of Europe and Asia, nesting among the birch woods and willow thickets and feeding on buds, seeds, fruits, and insects. Bramblings migrate southward for the winter, which they spend in the southern half of Europe and the Middle East. Birds nesting in Siberia fly to Japan for the winter.

ORDER: Passeriformes
FAMILY: Fringillidae
SPECIES: *Fringilla montifringilla*

Bream

Sea bream include several fish more properly called WRASSES, but the name bream usually refers to a freshwater fish belonging to the CARP family. Freshwater bream are stocky, narrow-bodied fish living in slow-moving rivers and lakes throughout northern and eastern Europe. They generally grow to about 24 in. (60 cm) in length, but because they are so deep-bodied they can weigh up to 17 lb. (8 kg).

Bream are sluggish moving fish that feed on small creatures in the mud but occasionally snap up small fish.

In North America, bream are marine fish related to scups and porgies. The sea bream grows to about a foot (30 cm) in length and lives in the Caribbean and off the coast of Florida.

ORDER: Cypriniformes
FAMILY: Cyprinidae

Brine shrimp

The brine shrimp is a small crustacean, closely related to the FAIRY SHRIMP. It lives in salty lakes and pools, generally in water that is twice as salty as seawater. Although less than .4 in. (1 cm) long, these shrimp are often so abundant that the water appears red. The brine shrimp has two pairs of antennae, two compound eyes on stalks, and a third eye in the middle of its head. It has 11 pairs of limbs.

ORDER: Anostraca
SPECIES: *Artemia salina*

Bristlemouth

A type of small, deep-sea fish which, although not widely known, is probably the most common of all ocean fish. The reason for the obscurity of bristlemouth fish is that when they are fished out of the ocean depths, their flimsy bodies are so broken up by the net as to be almost unrecognizable.

Bristlemouths are small fish usually not more than 2 in. (5 cm) long. Owing to their skimpy skeletons and poorly developed muscles, they weigh very little. Bristlemouths, like many other deep-sea creatures, have rows of light organs on their bodies. These fish get their name from their wide gape and bristlelike teeth.

ORDER: Salmoniformes
FAMILY: Gonostomatidae

The **bream** is a deep-bodied fish with a high back.

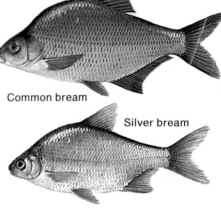

Common bream

Silver bream

Bristletail

The bristletails are primitive, wingless insects. There are two distinct groups – those with two "tails" and those with three. Two-tailed bristletails are very slender, soil-living insects. Their tails are usually narrow, but in some species they are stouter and sometimes resemble little pincers. Most feed on decaying plant material. Some of the three-tailed species live under stones on the seashore, but the best known are the domestic SILVERFISH and firebrat.

ORDERS: Diplura (two-tailed); Thysanura (three-tailed)

Bristleworm

The bristleworms form one of the main groups into which the segmented worms, or ANNELIDS, are divided. With few exceptions, the bristleworms are sea creatures. Most have cylindrical bodies, along which are a number of limb-like projections, called *parapodia*. Each parapodium carries bunches

Three kinds of **bristleworm**; the peacock worm and *Serpula vermicularis* live in tubes.

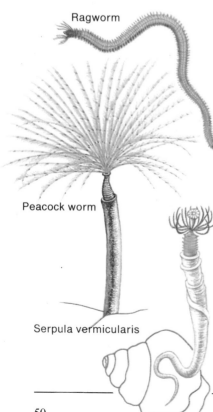

Ragworm

Peacock worm

Serpula vermicularis

Although the **brown bear** is a carnivore, it eats berries and other plant material.

of bristles. There are more than 5,000 species of bristleworms, ranging in length from a fraction of an inch (1 cm) to more than 20 ft. (6 m). Colors range from dull brown to pink, red, and green.

Some bristleworms live in tubes in the seabed, while others move around, swimming or crawling under shells and rocks. Bristleworms feed on particles of plant and animal matter which they filter from the water or mud, though some are active carnivores. A few are parasites of other marine creatures. Familiar bristle-worms include the LUGWORMS and ragworms used as bait by fishermen, and sea mice, which are not really wormlike in shape and have a feltlike covering of short bristles over their backs.

CLASS: Polychaeta

Brittlestar

These ECHINODERMS look like slender STARFISH, with five snakelike arms joined to a central disk, or body. These arms break off easily, but the animal can regrow them. They are covered with rows of hard plates and spines. On the underside of each arm are tube feet, which are used for feeding. Brittlestars feed on small particles of animal and plant life, and also on larger animals. They normally move around by "rowing" through the seabed mud with their arms.

CLASS: Ophiuroidea
ORDER: Ophiurida

Brown bear

There is uncertainty as to whether there are many species of brown bear or only one. However, most zoologists now believe that there is only one species, of which there are several races of subspecies.

The European brown bear once roamed all over Europe and Asia, but its European range is now confined to parts of the Pyrenees, Swiss Alps, Carpathians, Balkans, Norway, Sweden, and Finland. It is 5 to 7.5 ft. (1.5 to 2.4 m) long and weighs 200 to 775 lb. (91 to 349 kg).

The grizzly bear is the North American race of brown bear, and is larger than the European race. Like other bears, it was once widely distributed, but is now mostly confined to northern Canada. It is said to have poor eyesight, but its sense of smell is acute. The Kodiak bear is the largest of the brown bears, being about 10 ft (3 m) long and weighing 1,540 to 1,760 lb. (700 to 800 kg).

It is found mainly on Kodiak

Island, off the coast of Alaska.

Brown bears live in wild, mountainous country, wandering around singly or in family groups. Their home ranges have an average radius of 18 miles (30 km) or more. They are not normally aggressive, but can be very dangerous if aroused. Most attacks are made by injured bears or females separated from their cubs. Grizzly bears have the greatest reputation for fierceness, but the enormous and powerful Kodiak bear is truly terrifying when angry. It is said to be able to kill a horse or an ox with one blow of its forepaw.

Like other bears, brown bears eat a wide variety of both plant and animal food. Among other things they are highly skilled at fishing – standing patiently in shallow water and scooping up fish as they swim by. They are particularly partial to salmon.

Their breeding habits are similar to those of BLACK BEARS. They mate in June and the cubs, weighing 1.1 to 1.5 lb. (.5 to .7 kg), are born in January, during the winter sleep.

ORDER: Carnivora
FAMILY: Ursidae
SPECIES: *Ursus arctos*

Brown butterfly

The browns are a large group of butterflies. They are called this because most of the several hundred species are mostly brown. The most obvious feature, however, is the possession of a number of prominent eye spots around the edges of the wings. These eye spots are simply patterns, each consisting of a light ring with a dark center, and they act as decoys. Birds see the spots and peck at them instead of attacking the butterfly's body. The insect is not harmed and is able to fly away with no more than a small piece cut out of its wing. There are some very large members in the family, but most of the browns are medium-sized butterflies, with the females often larger and paler than the males. They are found mainly on grassland and heathland or in light woodland. Quite a number of species have also made their homes on mountaintops, especially in the Alps and Pyrenees. The caterpillars feed almost exclusively on grasses. Familiar European species include the meadow brown, the ringlet, and the wall brown. The family also includes the marbled white. This is white, with black or brown marbling, but it still has the characteristic eye spots of the browns. In North America, the brown butterflies are variously known as nymphs and satyrs. Two common species are the common wood nymph and the pearly eye.

ORDER: Lepidoptera
FAMILY: Satyridae

Budgerigar (Parakeet)

The budgerigar or parakeet is an Australian member of the parrot family. It lives in the desert parts of Australia, traveling in large flocks from one feeding ground to

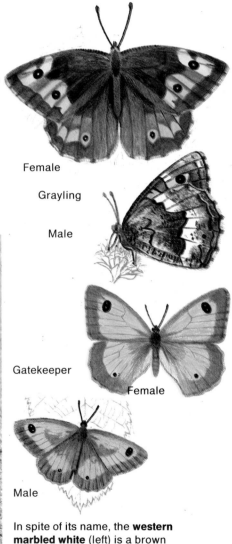

Female

Grayling

Male

Gatekeeper

Female

Male

In spite of its name, the **western marbled white** (left) is a brown butterfly. The **grayling** (above) is common in many places.

another except in the breeding season. Budgerigars eat seeds and fruit, and are a threat to grain crops. They nest in trees, carving out nest holes in rotten wood.

Wild budgerigars are grass-green with bright yellow on the head and long tapering blue tails. The upper parts are barred and scalloped with black and yellow, and there is a blue patch on each cheek and three black spots on each side of the throat. The base of the bill is blue in males and brownish in females.

Budgerigars are popular as pets, and selective breeding has produced many colored varieties, including darker shades of green, blue, yellow, gray, and olive. The birds readily mimic other sounds in captivity, including human speech.

ORDER: Psittaciformes
FAMILY: Psittacidae
SPECIES: *Melopsittacus undulatus*

Bugs

The bugs are an immense group of insects ranging from tiny APHIDS and SCALE INSECTS to large CICADAS and giant WATER BUGS that are 4 in. (10 cm) long. Their habits are equally wide ranging, but they all possess needlelike mouthparts which they plunge into plants or other animals to suck their juices. There are two distinct sections within the group – the Heteropetera and the Homoptera. Some experts consider these to be separate orders, while others put them into a single order known as the Hemiptera. Heteropteran bugs may be winged or wingless, but when wings are present there is a tough, horny base part and a membranous tip to each front wing. The hind wings are completely membrane. The wings are folded flat over the body at rest and, unlike beetle *elytra*, they overlap each other. Heteropteran bugs include both sap-sucking and carnivorous species, and many live in the water.

Homopteran bugs are all sap-feeders and they live on land. The front wings may be tough, or they may be membranous, but they are always of a uniform texture. They are usually held rooflike over the body at rest. The antennae are usually very small and bristlelike, although they are quite long in the aphids. Many of the homopteran bugs can jump, and are known as hoppers.

All the bugs grow up through nymphal stages which resemble the adults, and there is no chrysalis stage. There are well over 50,000 species.

ORDER: Hemiptera

A red-whiskered **bulbul**; Bulbuls often form large, noisy flocks.

Bulbul   N, V

The name given to members of a family of 119 species of small birds that live in the warmer parts of Europe, Asia, and Africa. They have also been introduced to other countries such as New Zealand and the United States. They range from the size of a house sparrow to the size of a blackbird. Generally dull in color, the sexes are usually similar. Some species have bright patches of red, yellow, or white.

Out of the breeding season bulbuls live in noisy flocks. They are mostly forest-dwellers.

ORDER: Passeriformes
FAMILY: Pycnonotidae

Bullfinch

A brightly colored FINCH found across Europe and Asia from the British Isles to Japan. It generally inhabits woodlands. Bullfinches feed on buds and seeds, causing enormous damage to fruit trees as they work their way along the branches from the tips, stripping the buds as they go. They do this after their supply of seeds has been

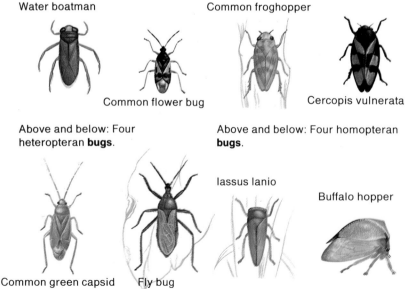

Water boatman

Common flower bug

Above and below: Four heteropteran **bugs**.

Common green capsid   Fly bug

Common froghopper

Cercopis vulnerata

Above and below: Four homopteran **bugs**.

Iassus lanio

Buffalo hopper

A male **bullfinch** displays his splendid breast.

exhausted. Their nests are made of fine twigs with moss and lichen and are built in hedgerows. There may be three clutches of four to five eggs.

ORDER: Passeriformes
FAMILY: Fringillidae
SPECIES: *Pyrrhula pyrrhula*

Bullfrog

This large North American frog can grow up to 8 in. (20 cm) in length. Bullfrogs seldom leave water except in very wet weather. They lie along the water's edge, and pounce on passing worms or insects. But bullfrogs take much larger prey as well. A big bullfrog can gobble up baby turtles, small snakes, mice, and ducklings. Even swallows flying by may be snatched from the air.

ORDER: Anura
FAMILY: Ranidae
SPECIES: *Rana catesbeiana*

Bullhead

The bullhead is a freshwater fish living in European rivers. How-ever, the name bullhead is also given to a number of other small freshwater and marine fish living in various parts of the world.

In North America, relatives of the bullhead are known as SCULPINS, and the term bullhead is applied to the CATFISH. In the southern United States a marine fish of the Sciaenidae family is also called bullhead.

The European bullhead is 2.8 to 6 in. (7 to 15 cm) long with a broad, flat head that is rounded in front, and a body stout in the head region and tapering to the tail. Its color is normally greenish-yellow with dark bars and blotches, but the bullhead can change its color patterns to match those of the stony riverbed on which it is lying. Also it may change color as a result of fear or rage.

The bullhead is a highly aggressive little fish which will nip any unwary finger and for this reason it has been a source of fun to children. It seeks the cover of stones and when disturbed darts away to fresh cover with such speed as to be practically invisible. Bullheads feed mostly at night, mainly on insects but also on anything else that comes along, including fish as big as or even bigger than itself. The sharp spines on its gill covers give it protection against all but the largest preda-tors. A HERON can manage a bull-head easily, but a GREBE, which does not have the trick of turning the fish to swallow it headfirst, may well choke on a bullhead's gill cover spines.

ORDER: Scorpaeniformes
FAMILY: Cottidae

White-tailed bumblebee (queen)

Bumblebee

These large, hairy, black and yellow bees are found in most temperate regions, buzzing around flowers in summer. Like the HONEYBEES, they are social in-sects, although their colonies are generally smaller and less complex – between 50 and several hundred members. Unlike honeybees, only the queen lives through the winter, and bumblebees do not die when they sting.

A bumblebee colony begins in spring when the queen emerges from hibernation. She builds a nest with moss and grass on, or under, the ground (old mouse holes are popular), and stocks it with pollen and nectar from nearby flowers. This is mixed to form "bee bread." Wax secreted from the queen's *abdomen* is used to make individual chambers or cells in which she lays her eggs and stores the food supply. The eggs develop into larvae, then pupate within a week or two. Young bumblebees, called workers, emerge. Some leave the nest to help the queen collect further sup-plies of pollen and nectar, while others build more wax cells to enlarge the colony. Later the colony rears drones and queens.

Bumblebees are farmers' best friends because they pollinate, or help to fertilize, many plants such as clover which are important as

Below: A **bumblebee** sips nectar. Bumblebees form colonies, but these are smaller than those of honeybees.

food for livestock. They have developed long tongues for sipping the sweet liquid nectar found deep within flowers. As they do this, tiny grains of pollen stick to their hairy legs and bodies. When they visit other flowers, some of the pollen brushes off and fertilizes the flowers. The rest of the pollen is carried back to the nest with the nectar, which is regurgitated and mixed with enzymes to change it into honey. Unlike honeybees, they do not produce enough honey to be collected by humans.

ORDER: Hymenoptera
FAMILY: Apidae

Bunting   N, R

A name used in the Old World for a group of finchlike birds which live mostly in open country. The best-known North American species is the indigo bunting. The painted bunting lives in the Southeastern U.S. It is about 6 inches (15 cm) long. The lazuli bunting lives in Canada and the Western U.S. Old World buntings occur throughout Europe, most of Asia, and large parts of Africa. Examples are the yellow-hammer, reed bunting, and the corn bunting.

A **burnet moth** displays narrow wings brightly patched with color.

Corn bunting

Male (summer)

Female

Male (winter)

Reed bunting

Many buntings are migratory, moving south in the autumn and returning to their northern breeding grounds in the spring. Outside the breeding season many buntings form flocks. They feed on seeds, especially those of grasses, and on insects and their larvae.

ORDER: Passeriformes
FAMILY: Emberizidae

Burnet moth

The burnets are brightly colored, day-flying moths found mainly in grassy places. Black and red are the main colors, but close examination reveals that the front wings of many species are a deep metallic green, especially when the insects are freshly emerged from their pupae. The bold colors warn birds and other predators that the bur-

nets are unpleasant to eat; in fact, they contain a form of cyanide in their bodies. The antennae are markedly thicker at the tips, but there is no risk of confusing these insects with butterflies because of their very narrow front wings. Although they beat their wings rapidly, they fly slowly and appear to drift from flower to flower. The larvae feed on various low-growing plants and pupate in papery cocoons on grass stems.

ORDER: Lepidoptera
FAMILY: Zygaenidae

Burrowing owl

The little burrowing owl was once common on the prairies of North

America, but the spread of agriculture has reduced its numbers. Only 9 in. (23 cm) high, it is unusual among owls in that it hunts by day as well as by night, pouncing on small rodents and insects. It nests in a burrow, usually taking over a hole made by some other animal, although it can dig by scraping with its talons. The eggs are laid at the end of the burrow and guarded by the parents. Burrowing owls used to breed in colonies, but most of these have disappeared.

ORDER: Strigiformes
FAMILY: Strigidae
SPECIES: *Speotyto cunicularia*

Burying beetle

The burying beetles, also called sexton beetles, feed on, and breed in, the dead bodies of small animals. Males and females usually work in pairs, and they bury the carrion by scraping the soil away from underneath it. If the soil is too hard where the beetles find the carcass, they may drag it to a more convenient place. Some are jet black, but the most familiar species carry bright orange bands on their *elytra*. Having buried a carcass, the female lays her eggs beside it. The grubs that hatch out feed partly on the decaying meat, and partly on the fly larvae and other scavengers that feed there.

ORDER: Coleoptera
FAMILY: Silphidae

Burying beetles

Bushbaby (Galago)   N, V

The bushbaby, also called the galago, is an agile, nocturnal animal. It leaps easily from branch to branch and a standing jump of

7.5 ft. (225 cm) has been recorded. There are five species, all of which occur in Africa south of the Sahara. The most widespread, the Senegal bushbaby, is 16 in. (40 cm) long, including the tail. It has a round head, with large eyes and a short muzzle. The ears are large and the fur ranges from yellowish-gray to brown. The hind legs are longer than the front legs. The ends of a bushbaby's fingers and toes are flattened with pads of thick skin on the underside that help it get a grip on the smooth bark of the trees from which it gets its food – insects, especially locusts, fruit and birds' eggs, as well as flowers, pollen, and honey.

Unusually for a large animal, the bushbaby pollinates plants. Thicktailed bushbabies feed on the newly opened flowers of the baobab tree, eating only the outer parts of the flowers, so that no damage is caused to seed or fruit production. As they feed they pick up the pollen on their snouts which they then transfer to the next flower, so pollinating it.

ORDER: Primates
FAMILY: Lorisidae

Bushbuck

The bushbuck is an antelope, closely related to the NYALA and KUDU, which inhabits the forests and bush of Africa south of the Sahara. It stands up to 30 in. (76 cm) at the shoulder and weighs between 100 and 170 lb. (45 and

The **bushbuck** is a small antelope that lives in the forest and bush of southern Africa.

77 kg). The color of the back and flanks ranges from a light tawny in females to a dark brown in the larger males, with white spots and stripes. The sharp horns of the male may reach 22 in. (56 cm). Females may also have horns but are generally hornless. The horns are used to fight off predators. Bushbuck have been known to kill leopards, wild dogs, and, when wounded, even men.

ORDER: Artiodactyla
FAMILY: Bovidae
SPECIES: *Tragelaphus scriptus*

Bush cricket   N, V, Ex

Bush crickets are often confused with GRASSHOPPERS, but they can be distinguished very easily by their long *antennae*, often much longer than the body. Female bush crickets are also easily identified by their curved, saberlike *ovipositor*. Bush crickets are much more nocturnal than grasshoppers

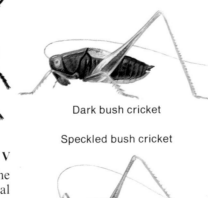

Dark bush cricket

Speckled bush cricket

Great green bush cricket

The great green **bush cricket** above sings loudly in long bursts.

and, as the name suggests, prefer shrubs and hedgerows. Some, such as the great green bush cricket, are fully winged and fly well, while others are quite flightless. The tizi, from southern Europe, is a well-known flightless species. Some American species, known as katydids, are noted for their loud songs. The insects seem to be calling, "Katy-did, Katy-did," hence their name. Katydids can be heard most often in late summer and the autumn. Male bush crickets sing by rubbing their wing bases together, and even the flightless species have enough wing to produce their calls. These are often much higher pitched than grasshoppers calls. Bush crickets eat both plant and animal matter, but small insects are their main source of food. There are thousands of species and they are especially numerous in the tropics.
ORDER: Orthoptera
FAMILY: Tettigoniidae

Bushmaster

The bushmaster is the largest poisonous snake found in the Americas. It can be up to 12 ft. (3.7 m) long and is the only American PIT VIPER to lay eggs. Another unusual feature is the small, silent "rattle" at the end of the tail. This earns the snake its name *muta*, meaning "silent."

This snake occurs in northern South America and Central America. Its pale brown body marked with dark brown blotches conceals it in its forest habitat. Its bite is deadly, but is seldom used on people.
ORDER: Squamata
FAMILY: Crotalidae
SPECIES: *Lachesis muta*

Bush pig

The bush pig lives in mostly broken country in Africa south of the Sahara and in Madagascar. The bush pig can run fast, swim well and shows spirited defense against intruders, such as its main predator, the leopard. Although it is a sensitive, shy animal, it is a menace to farmers because of the damage it does to crops. The bush pig is stout-bodied, with a large head, and a coat of short bristles. Young adults are reddish, but older animals become reddish-brown or black. The height at the shoulder averages 30 in. (76 cm) and the pig can weigh up to 300 lb. (136 kg). There are two pairs of tusks which are more apparent when the mouth is open. The upper tusk is 3 in. (8 cm) long and the lower one is 7.5 in. (19 cm) long.
ORDER: Artiodactyla
FAMILY: Suidae
SPECIES: *Potamochoerus porcus*

Bustard   N, R, V, E

A group of large birds 1.2 to 4.4 ft. (36 to 132 cm) in length. Bustards are birds of open country, such as plains, downs and deserts, where their mottled gray or brown plumage camouflages them and they can run freely on their powerful legs. There are 22 species of bustard, spread across the Old World from the Canary Islands to Australia, although most species live in Africa. Many of them now have a reduced range because of overhunting.

Bustards are noted for their striking courtship displays. The male great bustard undergoes a remarkable transformation when

Little **bustards**

Male

Female

Right: A female **bush cricket**; note the saberlike ovipositor.

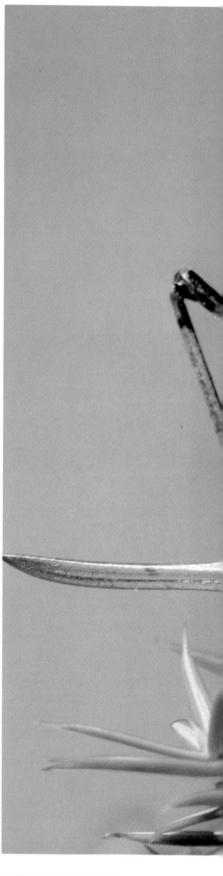

it displays. From being a dull gray and brown bird, it suddenly becomes a billowing mass of white feathers. The feathers on the back are turned over, and the tail is turned up and over the back, to display the white undersides. The nest is merely some trampled grass or a depression in the ground.

ORDER: Gruiformes
FAMILY: Otididae

Butcherbird

The name butcherbird is given to six species of birds from Australia and New Guinea which impale their prey on thorns or even barbed wire. They belong to the same family as the currawongs and bell magpies, and bear some resemblance to CROWS and SHRIKES. They have large heads and hooked, shrikelike bills. Shrikes are also sometimes referred to as butcherbirds. Butcherbirds stay paired throughout the year. They are shy birds but are noted for their song.

ORDER: Passeriformes
FAMILY: Cracticidae

Butterflies and moths

With over 150,000 known species, the butterflies and moths form one of the largest of the insect orders. They range from huge ATLAS MOTHS and BIRDWING BUTTERFLIES, with wingspans exceeding 10 in. (25 cm), to ones barely a tenth of an inch. (3 mm) across the wings. Apart from a few wingless female moths, the insects all have four wings which are clothed with tiny scales. These give the wings their colors and patterns, but they rub off quite easily and older insects often lose much of their color. The insects feed almost entirely on nectar, although some butterflies also enjoy the juices of ripe fruit and even those of rotting meat. The liquids are sucked up through a long tongue, or *proboscis*, which acts like a drinking straw. The tongues of some moths are several inches long, so

Note the feathery antennae of an elegant North American **moon moth**.

the insects can reach the nectar in deep-throated flowers – often while hovering in front of the flowers. When not in use, the proboscis is coiled up like a watch spring under the head. A number of moths have no proboscis and do not feed·in the adult state. One small group actually has functional jaws and feeds by chewing pollen. No more than .5 in. (13 mm) across their metallic wings, these little insects are quite common in the spring.

The division of the order into butterflies and moths is a very unequal one, and also a very artificial one. The butterflies account for roughly 20,000 species, arranged in no more than a dozen families, and there is the same degree of difference between a butterfly and a HAWK MOTH as there is between that same hawk moth and a CLOTHES MOTH. The division was used by the early naturalists, who called brightly colored, day-flying species butterflies, and the duller, nocturnal species moths, but this distinction is not valid in every case. The BURNET MOTHS, for example, are brilliantly colored, day-flying insects. There is no one difference between all the moths and all the butterflies, although most of the temperate species can be distinguished without much difficulty. Most butterflies have clubbed *an-*

A butterfly's lifecycle.

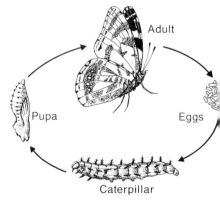

Adult

Eggs

Caterpillar

Pupa

Peacock butterfly

Peacock caterpillar

Camberwell beauty

Above: A narrow-bordered bee hawk moth, showing its striking resemblance to a bumblebee.

Broad-bordered bee hawk moth

Red admiral

Left: A magnified photograph of a section of a butterfly's wing.

tennae, but few of the moths show this feature; their antennae are usually threadlike or feathery. The burnets have clubbed antennae, but to distinguish these from butterflies it is only necessary to look under the wings. Springing from the "shoulder" of the hind wing there is a stout bristle, called the *frenulum*. It sticks forward and latches into a little clip on the front wing. Its purpose is to hold the two wings together in flight. Most moths have a frenulum, but butterflies do not. Their wings are held together by a large overlap.

Males and females find each other by sight or by scent, and often by a combination of the two. The scent may be emitted by the female, as in many SILK MOTHS and EMPEROR MOTHS, or by the male, as in many butterflies. The males of the emperor and silk moths are so sensitive to the female scent that they can find females from up to a mile away. After mating, the female lays her eggs, usually placing them in batches on the correct food plant for the resulting *larvae*, or caterpillars. She uses her feet to "taste" the plant first and make sure that it is suitable. Most caterpillars are fussy about their food and are restricted to just one food plant or a group of closely related plants. Most feed freely on leaves, but some tunnel into stems and fruits, and some eat roots. Larvae of the pigmy moths are so small that they can spend their lives tunneling between the upper and lower surfaces of leaves. The larvae of the CLOTHES MOTHS are unusual in that they eat wool and other animal material.

All caterpillars have biting mouths, quite unlike the *probosci* of the adults. They have three pairs of true legs at the front, and two to five pairs of fleshy *prolegs* farther back. Most species molt four times, and then they are ready to pupate. It is during the pupal stage that the caterpillar's body is converted into that of the adult. Most moth larvae pupate in underground chambers or spin silken cocoons among the vegetation or the debris on the ground. SKIPPER BUTTERFLIES make flimsy *cocoons*, but most other butterflies have naked pupae, or *chrysalises*. These may hang upside down from the food plants, or they may be attached in an upright position to suitable stems or fences and held in place by a silken girdle. The caterpillar produces the silken supports before changing into the chrysalis. The chrysalis stage may last several weeks, or throughout the winter. When the adult is ready to emerge, its wing patterns can be seen through the chrysalis wall. The wings are soft and crumpled at first, but they soon expand and harden and the insect can fly away.

ORDER: Lepidoptera

Butterfly fish

Butterfly fish is the name given to many different kinds of saltwater fish, but it is most descriptive of the one species of freshwater butterfly fish, which lives in West African rivers. Measuring only 4 in. (10 cm) long, this fish has several characteristics which can

Copperbanded
butterfly fish

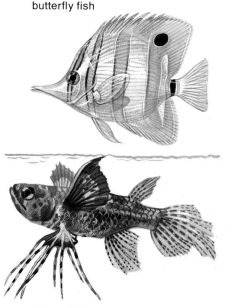

be compared with a butterfly's, most particularly its large, delicate *pectoral fins* which are spread like wings and which allow the butterfly fish to fly or glide over the surface of the water. Its other fins, which may act as stabilizers in flight, are also large and winglike or rudderlike.

The butterfly fish is a surface-swimmer, with a boat-shaped body flattened at the top, and a mouth that faces upward. Its color is gray-green to silver-brown and its body is marked with spots and streaks. It is an unlikely relative of the giant ARAPAIMA of South American rivers.

ORDER: Osteoglossiformes
FAMILY: Pantodontidae

The freshwater **butterfly fish** (left) lives in West African rivers. It is a surface-dweller with large pectoral fins resembling outspread butterfly wings. The copperbanded butterfly fish is one of many marine fish of this name.

Buzzards (left and above) are well known for their effortless, gliding flight.

Buzzard

The common buzzard of Europe is one of a number of large HAWKS bearing this name. Buzzards resemble EAGLES in their soaring flight. All are large birds, with wing spans of up to 5 ft. (1.5 m). In flight, buzzards spiral effortlessly with their broad wings outstretched, rising in the thermals (warm air currents) for great distances. They can thus fly long distances without wasting energy flapping their wings, and buzzards migrate using this technique. In the United States, the term buzzard is applied more commonly to vultures, whereas members of the genus *Buteo* are called hawks.

Buzzards hunt by pouncing on animals on the ground. They sit motionless on a favorite perch, scanning the ground with their keen eyes, or hover in midair. They feed mainly on rabbits, voles, mice, and lizards. After courtship, during which the male and female indulge in graceful aerobatics, a large bowl-shaped nest is made in a tree or on a rock ledge. Normally two eggs are laid, but up to six have been recorded.

ORDER: Falconiformes
FAMILY: Accipitridae
SPECIES: *Buteo buteo*

C

Cabbage white butterfly

The cabbage white, also known as the large white, is a serious pest of cabbages and related plants in many parts of the world. The adult is an attractive white insect with black markings, and the female lays batches of yellow eggs on the food plants in spring and summer. The black and yellow caterpillars eat the leaves and then pupate on convenient walls and fences. Relatively few become adult butterflies, however, because a little ICHNEUMON fly attacks many of the caterpillars. Shriveled caterpillar skins are very common in late summer, with clusters of yellow ichneumon cocoons around them. The closely related small white is an even worse pest, as it is found almost all over the world. The cabbage white butterfly was introduced into North America from Europe about 1860.

ORDER: Lepidoptera
FAMILY: Pieridae
SPECIES: *Pieris brassicae* (cabbage white); *Pieris rapae* (small white)

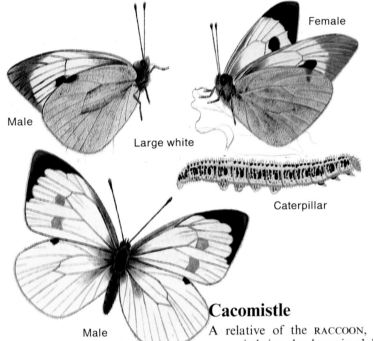

Male

Large white

Female

Caterpillar

Male

The **large white** and **small white** butterflies are serious pests. The caterpillars eat vast quantities of food plants.

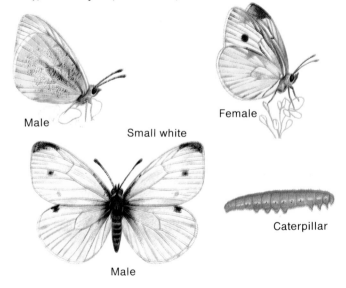

Male

Small white

Female

Caterpillar

Male

Cacomistle

A relative of the RACCOON, the cacomistle is a slender animal. It is up to 30 in. (76 cm) long, of which 17 in. (43 cm) is a bushy tail ringed black and white, and weighs only about 2.2 lb. (1 kg). The coat is grayish-buff, darker along the back, with white underparts. It is found in the southern and western parts of the United States and in Mexico.

The cacomistle is a shy, nocturnal animal. It sleeps by day in a den among rocks and emerges at night to feed on small rodents, birds, lizards, and insects. It is an agile tree-climber.

ORDER: Carnivora
FAMILY: Procyonidae
SPECIES: *Bassariscus astutus*

Caddis fly

The caddis flies are mostly small or medium-sized mothlike insects, whose wings are clothed with fine hairs. Most are black or brown in color, and they usually rest with

Continued on page 64

Camouflage

Unless they have special means of defense or escape, animals must conceal themselves from their enemies. One way is to merge with the color of their surroundings. Where such resemblance is useful, natural selection has produced beautifully adapted animals. The mainly brown grazing animals merge with the plains where they feed – especially when one remembers that their enemies – lions and the like – see only in shades of gray. This general color resemblance, however, is only part of the answer. A solid body will tend to stand out in relief against the background of shading effects.

A great many animals have darker colors on the top surface than underneath. This is called countershading. In nature, the light usually comes from above and there is shadow below. This effect is countered by the coloration of the body and the result is that all shadows disappear and the animal merges as a flat shape into the background. Countershading is prominent among the grazing mammals where it is produced by gradation of color or by patterns that change lower down the body. The zebra's stripes and the giraffe's pattern, for instance, produce countershading when seen at a distance. These patterns are also disruptive.

Disruptive coloring is another very important feature of animal life. Contrasting colors and patterns break up the outline of the body and draw attention away from the

In the center of the picture a **lappet moth** is perfectly **camouflaged** as a dead leaf.

whole shape. Although an animal with disruptive coloring may look obvious close to, or out of its natural surroundings, against a natural background it may completely disappear. Fish, snakes, and many ground-nesting birds make use of this type of coloration.

The CHAMELEON employs a different method of color camouflage. If a dark colored chameleon is put on a leafy branch, it will seem to disappear from sight in about 15 minutes. It is one of a number of animals that gain protection by changing their colors to blend in with the background. The color change is a natural process involving redistribution of *pigments* in the skin.

Most of the animals that can change their colors have the pigments in special color cells called chromatophores.

This **bush cricket** has the color, shape, and texture of the leaf on which it perches.

Chromatophores respond to light and, to a lesser degree, temperature. Although in some animals the actual color cells expand and contract, it is more common for the pigment to be withdrawn into the center of the cell or spread out along the branches.

There are two types of color cell response. One, known as direct, or primary response, is caused by light falling on the cells themselves. Strong light causes the pigment to contract and the overall color of the animal becomes pale.

The other type of response – indirect or secondary – is via the eyes and the brain. When the eyes detect a dark background, messages arrive at the color cells, causing them to expand and produce a darker coloration. A light background similarly produces a contrac-

tion of the pigments. The messages to the color cells may be in the form of direct nerve impulses from the brain. Alternatively, the brain may cause the release of *hormones* that act on the color cells. In many animals, both nerve and hormone messages are concerned with the control of the color cells.

Flatfish such as the flounder are well known for their color-changing ability. They contain black pigment together with others ranging from yellow to red. Combinations of these are enough to produce a likeness to the majority of natural backgrounds. Flatfish can even produce a reasonable copy of a chess board pattern if the colors are available in its skin.

A different form of camouflage involves the resemblance of an animal to its surroundings. Some of the best examples are to be found among the insects. Many

butterflies, although they may be brightly colored on the upper side, resemble leaves when at rest. Stick insects and leaf insects are other well-known examples. Several species of treehopper are almost indistinguishable from thorns when sitting on the appropriate twigs, and various caterpillars resemble twigs themselves. Some sea horses are disguised so well that they completely disappear against a background of seaweed.

Mimicry is the name given to the cases where an animal benefits from resembling another animal rather than its surroundings. Among so many species of insect, it happens that a number of them look alike. If one species is protected – by an evil smell, sting, or warning colors – other similar-looking ones will also derive benefit. The resemblance will then be continued and improved by natural selection over many generations.

Nature designed this caterpillar to look like a twig.

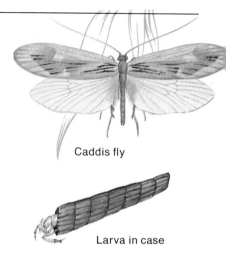

Caddis fly

Larva in case

Left: A **caddis fly** in its typical resting position, with antennae pointing to the front.

the wings held rooflike over the body and the *antennae* held straight out in front. There are nearly 6,000 known species, and with few exceptions they spend their early lives in the water. Some larvae live freely in the ponds and streams, catching and eating an assortment of small animals. Some species that live in running water actually spin silken fishing nets among the plants to trap plant debris and small animals for food. Caddis *larvae* are best known, however, for the portable cases that most of them build to protect their soft bodies. Sand grains, small snail shells, pieces of stick, and leaf fragments are all used to build these tubular cases on frameworks of silk. Each species has its own special design. Some actually fix their cases to large stones. Case-building larvae are generally plant-eaters or scavengers. The larvae pupate in the cases, and the pupae can actually swim to the surface to allow the adults to escape. Most adults remain close to the water and rarely feed.
ORDER: Trichoptera

Caiman   N, E

Caimans are closely related to ALLIGATORS. One difference is that some caimans have belly skin that is reinforced with bony plates. All five caiman species live in northern South America, and one occurs as far north as southern Mexico. The smallest species is the dwarf caiman, up to 4 ft. (1.2 m) long. The largest is the black caiman, up to 15 ft. (4.6 m) long.
ORDER: Crocodilia
FAMILY: Alligatoridae

Camel   N, V

Camels are invaluable animals to the desert people of Asia and Africa. They provide the chief

Arabian **camels** are taking in water. The hump contains fat as a reserve of energy.

means of transportation and are an important source of food, clothing, and shelter.

There are two species: the one-humped, or Arabian, camel, and the Bactrian, or two-humped camel. Bactrian camels have shorter legs and are heavier than Arabian camels. Arabian camels, most of which live in Africa, are not generally wild, although there are herds which have descended from escaped domestic animals. But Bactrian camels, which are confined to Asia, have survived in the wild in the Gobi Desert in Central Asia. Gobi camels are active by day and are extremely shy. They live in groups consisting of one male and about five females.

Camels have long legs, a long neck, coarse hair, and tufted tails. Their feet have two toes, united by a tough web, with nails and tough, padded soles. A camel stands up to 6 ft. (1.8 m) at the shoulder and weighs up to 1,100 lb. (500 kg). The hump may weigh 100 lb. (45 kg). It contains fat, a reserve of energy.

The camel is well adapted to life in deserts. Its long eyelashes protect the eyes from windblown sand and its nostrils are easily closed. The feet are broad and enable the camel to walk easily over soft sand. The form of its body, with long neck and legs, provide a large surface area relative to the body's volume, which allows for easy loss of heat. But its best-known adaptation is the ability to go for long periods with very little food and drink. The camel sweats little and this helps it retain water. It gets water by eating desert plants, but it can go on a totally dry diet for several weeks, although it will steadily lose water. It is able to lose up to one-quarter of its body weight in water without showing signs of distress. Thirsty camels have been known to drink 100 qt. (100 l) of water or more in ten minutes. The water passes from the stomach into the body tissues and, after such a drink the body appears swollen.
ORDER: Artiodactyla

FAMILY: Camelidae
SPECIES: *Camelus dromedarius* (Arabian); *Camelus bactrianus* (Bactrian)

Canada goose

The Canada goose is the most widespread and best-known goose in North America. It is a large, gray-brown goose with a black head, neck, and tail and a white patch on the chin. Canada geese live in Alaska, Canada, and the northern United States. In winter they migrate as far south as the Gulf of Mexico. They prefer inland waters, although they are also found in estuaries and on coasts. Outside the breeding season they may form groups of 200 to 300.

Canada geese are mainly vegetarian. On land they graze grass, rushes, and sedges. In the sea they eat algae and eelgrass. They have favorite feeding grounds and generally congregate in areas where

The **Canada goose** is a North American bird that has been introduced to Europe.

food is abundant at a particular time of year. During the breeding season they eat small water animals as well as plants. They mate for life and the eggs are incubated in nests on the ground.
ORDER: Anseriformes
FAMILY: Anatidae
SPECIES: *Branta canadensis*

Canary

The canary is a member of the FINCH family, native to the Canary Islands, the Azores, and Madeira. It was imported into Europe in the 16th century and has since been bred to produce a number of colored varieties, from yellow, through orange, to those streaked with brown or black. Canaries live in bushes and clumps of trees, readily coming into gardens. Very popular as pet birds, canaries are noted for their song. In the wild, their main food is small seeds but they also eat leaf and fruit buds.
ORDER: Passeriformes
FAMILY: Fringillidae
SPECIES: *Serinus canaria*

Cape buffalo

By repute, the Cape buffalo is the most dangerous of African big game animals because it tends to charge whenever it is disturbed, and a charging buffalo is not easily stopped. Its only natural enemy is the lion, which it often kills in combat. The bulky, oxlike buffalo stands 4 to 5 ft. (122 to 152 cm) at the shoulder and the powerful adult bulls weigh nearly a ton. The head and shoulders are heavily built and the large horns spring from broad bases, sometimes meeting in the middle of the forehead and curving first down and then up, and finishing in a point. The longest horns recorded span 4.7 ft. (142 cm). The coat is brownish-black, and is thick in young buffaloes and sparse in older ones.

The Cape buffalo was once common throughout Africa south of the Sahara, but hunting and cattle disease have greatly reduced numbers in many places. Herds of 1,000 to 2,000 can still be seen in such places as Kruger National Park, South Africa.

ORDER: Artiodactyla
FAMILY: Bovidae
SPECIES: *Syncerus caffer*

Cape hunting dog

The cape hunting dog, or African wild dog, is a ferocious animal only distantly related to other members of the dog family. Unlike the others, it has only four toes on each foot – the dewclaw is missing. It stands about 2 ft. (60 cm) at the shoulder and measures up to 4 ft. (120 cm) from its nose to the tip of its bushy tail. Its coat is mottled black, yellow, and white.

Cape hunting dogs are found in the savanna of Africa, south of the Sahara Desert. They live in packs of 4 to 60 individuals and a pack usually remains in one area as long as food is abundant. Their prey consists of antelopes and other grazing animals – even large wildebeest. The pack hunts together in an organized manner. They can run long distances and will chase their prey until it collapses with exhaustion. Often, they begin tearing it to pieces before it is dead.

ORDER: Carnivora
FAMILY: Canidae
SPECIES: *Lycaon pictus*

Cape buffalo at a water hole.

Capercaillie

A large game bird of which there are two species. One lives in Scandinavia, Russia, and Central Europe, with isolated populations in the Pyrenees and Scotland. The second species lives in eastern Sibera. The male capercaillie is dark gray and nearly a yard (1 m) long. It has a spectacular court-ship display in which it raises its neck and fans out its tail. The female is smaller and brown, re-sembling a large GROUSE. Caper-caillies live in coniferous forests, and are able to survive the winter mainly by eating pine needles.

ORDER: Galliformes
FAMILY: Tetraonidae
SPECIES: *Tetrao urogallus* (Euro-pean); *Tetrao parvirostris* (Siber-ian)

The male **capercaillie** fans its tail when courting the female.

Male

Female

Capuchin

The capuchin is the once-familiar monkey of the organ grinder. It is an intelligent animal and popular in zoos and as a pet. Although there is still some dispute, most authorities now say that there are four species, belonging to the genus *Cebus*, and 33 subspecies. They live in troops in the forests of tropical South and Central America and fruit is their main

The **cardinal** is a familiar songbird of North America. The male's plumage is a bright red.

food. Capuchins are small mon-keys, measuring 12 to 15 in. (30 to 38 cm) long. Their tails, which may be 24 in. (60 cm) long, are used to grasp objects out of reach of the hands.

ORDER: Primates
FAMILY: Cebidae

Capybara

The capybara is the largest living rodent. It looks piglike, with hoof-like claws, a large short-eared head, and coarse brown hair. It may be over a yard (1 m) long and weigh up to 120 lb. (54 kg). A native of South America, it is always found near water. Capy-baras swim and dive well, using their slightly webbed feet as pad-dles. Their stored layers of fat give them natural buoyancy in the water. Capybaras eat water plants and grass, browsing in water or on grassland. If alarmed, the in-offensive capybara gallops for the safety of the nearest water.

ORDER: Rodentia
FAMILY: Hydrochoeridae
SPECIES: *Hydrochoerus hydro-choeris*

Caracal

This medium-sized cat has a short reddish coat, long legs, and long black ear tufts. Some zoologists consider it to be a true LYNX, while others see it as akin to the SERVAL. Caracals live in savanna and semi-desert throughout Africa and in parts of southern Asia as far east as India. They are becoming very scarce, and are extremely rare in Asia. They feed on a variety of animals, sometimes the prey being as large as a small antelope. Cara-cals are good jumpers, and will strike down birds that are already airborne by rearing up on their hind legs, or leaping up to 6.5 ft. (2 m) in the air. Young caracals are born in litters of 2 to 4 in an old aardvark burrow, fox hole, or hollow tree. Like any cat, the mother defends her young fiercely against intruders.

ORDER: Carnivora
FAMILY: Felidae
SPECIES: *Felis caracal*

Cardinal

A finchlike songbird that is found naturally in temperate parts of the United States. It has been intro-duced to Bermuda and Hawaii. In Hawaii it breeds year-round and has become a pest because of the damage it does to fruit trees. Apart from a black bib the plumage is a mixture of scarlets, the female being slightly duller.

ORDER: Passeriformes
FAMILY: Emberizidae
SPECIES: *Cardinalis cardinalis*

Cardinal fish

There are many different species of these small perchlike fish that live mainly on coral reefs in tropical seas. Like many other fish of this habitat, they have bright colors and patterns. Usually not more than 4 in. (10 cm) long, they ap-pear to be the main food of many larger fish of the reefs.

ORDER: Perciformes
FAMILY: Apogonidae

Caribou

The caribou belongs to the same species as REINDEER, but differs in several respects. Reindeer are domesticated or semidomesticated in Greenland, Scandinavia, and northern Russia, while caribou roam wild in North America and Siberia. Caribou have longer legs than reindeer. They stand 4 to 5 ft. (122 to 152 cm) at the shoulder and can weigh 700 lb. (318 kg). The coat varies from near black to almost white, but most caribou are brownish or grayish, with light underparts and rump. In winter, they become lighter and the hair lengthens. The ears and tail are short and the muzzle is furry. These winter changes reduce the amount of heat lost from the body in cold weather. Caribou and reindeer are the only deer in which both sexes bear antlers.

At the beginning of this century, there were probably about 1,750,000 caribou in northern Canada. The population then declined through overhunting, destruction of food by forest fires, and high mortality in severe weather. In 1955, the population was 278,900, but numbers have been increasing recently because of an intensive program of conservation.

Caribou crossing the tundra in Alaska. The annual migrations follow regular paths.

Caribou live in small bands of 5 to 100, or in herds of up to 3,000. In April and May, they migrate north to the open tundra, where they spend the summer. They winter in the woodlands at the southern end of their range. The annual migrations follow regular paths, which once made it easy for Native Americans to trap them. Caribou mate in late October to early November and the young are born in early June. Grizzly bears sometimes prey on young caribou, but wolves are their main enemy. Some northern Native Americans eat caribou meat.

ORDER: Artiodactyla
FAMILY: Cervidae
SPECIES: *Rangifer tarandus*

Carnivore

This name means "flesh-eater" and is applied to the cats and dogs and other members of the group of mammals called Carnivora. It is also used for meat-eaters in general.

These hunting flesh-eaters have evolved many different methods of catching their prey. Most cats stalk their prey slowly, and then pounce when they are near enough, using their large teeth to kill their victims. But CHEETAHS chase rapidly after their prey because they live on open plains and cannot stalk them unseen. WOLVES and hunting dogs also chase their prey, and often work together in packs. GOSHAWKS and PEREGRINES fly rapidly after smaller birds and snap them up in midair, while the DRAGONFLY does much the same to small insects. Good eyesight is obviously very important for these fast-moving predators.

A number of predatory animals actually shoot their prey. The SEA ANEMONES and their distant freshwater relative, HYDRA, fire poison "harpoons" which paralyze small animals swimming nearby. The anemone's tentacles then draw the prey into its mouth. The ARCHERFISH, from South-East Asia, fires small water droplets at insects flying just above the surface, snapping them up when they fall into the water. Perhaps the most amazing of all is the spitting spider, which approaches its victim and then fires two sticky threads from its jaws. The

Lions hunt in groups, creeping silently through the long grass. It is usually the lionesses that do the actual killing.

victim is pinned down by these threads and rendered completely helpless.

Many creatures, including the praying MANTIS and the TRAPDOOR SPIDER, ambush their prey and some animals actually set traps. The most famous of these trappers are the SPIDERS, whose delicate silken webs form deadly traps for flies and other small insects. Some webs are sticky, but others work simply by entangling the unfortunate insect. The spider is always nearby to administer a paralyzing bite and to wrap its victim in a silken shroud before sucking it dry. Some of the CADDIS larvae that live in fast-flowing water also spin silken snares. These are fairly simple nets suspended from water plants which trap debris and small animals.

Carp

The carp is the most widespread fish of the family to which it gives its name. Like its relative the GOLDFISH, the carp's original home was in the Far East, but it is now cultivated by people in many parts of the world. Carp live in the muddy bottoms of shallow waters where there are lots of water plants. They feed mainly on mud-dwelling animals. Sensory *barbels* under the mouth help in this hunting.

Carp have a reputation of long life, but this has often been greatly exaggerated. Perhaps a carp can live for as long as 50 years but 17 years is nearer the average life span. Similarly, their size is often exaggerated. Claims have been made for carp weighing 400 lb. (180 kg) but the largest authentic weight of a European carp is about 60 lb. (27 kg) for a fish over 1 yard (1 m) in length.

ORDER: Cypriniformes
FAMILY: Cyprinidae
SPECIES: *Cyprinus carpio*

The **carp** is a powerful fish that tests the angler's tackle to the full.

Cassowary

A large, timid bird of the rain forests of New Guinea and northern Australia. Cassowaries cannot fly, but they are well adapted to living in the dense undergrowth of the rain forests. The skin of their long neck and head is naked and brightly colored, but the body is covered with coarse, bristlelike black feathers. On the head is a bony casque, or helmet. The stiff plumage and bony helmet protect the cassowary as it runs through the undergrowth. Cassowaries are shy and secretive birds but, if cornered, they may leap and kick

out with their long, daggerlike claws. There are three species: the Australian cassowary, the one-wattled cassowary, and the Bennet's cassowary. The largest, the one-wattled cassowary, may be nearly 6 ft. (2 m) tall.
ORDER: Casuariiformes
FAMILY: Casuariidae

Cat

The domestic cat is a small member of the cat family, typically 30 in. (76 cm) long, including a 9 in. (23 cm) tail, and weighing up to 20 lb. (9.5 kg). Unlike wild cats, domesticated cats usually hold their tails horizontally when walking. Their claws can be drawn in and these they keep in condition by scratching at trees, posts, furniture, and carpets. They readily climb trees to escape dogs, to rob birds' nests, or to lie in the sun on branches. Long whiskers sprouting from the muzzle are probably used to feel the way in the dark. Coat color varies, although tabby markings (grayish-brown and black patterns, often striped) are dominant.

Cat hearing is acute. Cats can hear sounds above the range detected by the human ear: a cat beside a mousehole may hear rodent voices inaudible to us. Cats hunt silently, but in other situations produce a variety of sounds from the "meow" to the purr of pleasure. Male, or tom, cats seeking to impress a mate and deter rivals indulge in loud, insistent yowling.

There are more than 30 breeds of domestic cat, some longhaired like the Persian, but most short-haired like the Burmese. Several races of short-tailed cats exist, especially in Southeast Asia, and there are also tailless cats, such as

the Manx cat. Domestic breeds are probably a mixture of two wild species: the European wild cat and the African bush cat. The bush cat was tamed in ancient Egypt more than 3,000 years ago.
ORDER: Carnivora
FAMILY: Felidae
SPECIES: *Felis catus*

Catfish

The name of any of several hundred species of fish, all of which have whiskerlike *barbels* around the mouth. They fall into two groups: ARMORED CATFISH, which are discussed under that heading, and naked catfish, described here.

Naked catfish have an amazing variety of forms and habits. The European catfish, or wels, is a large, flattened fish with very long whiskers, which eats frogs and fish. It can grow to a length of 8 ft. (2.7 m) or more. The banjo catfish of South America have very flat bodies and long, thin tails which give them their name. Another family of marine catfish, Ploto-sidae, contains one of the most dangerous fish of the coral reefs, with poisonous spines that can inflict fatal wounds. Equally to be feared are tiny catfish of South American rivers which are parasites that enter body cavities and cause severe internal wounds.

Some small African catfish are natural clowns, often swimming upside down. In the mating season the males and females, in this position, repeatedly swim at one another and collide head-on.
ORDER: Siluriformes

The wels is a **catfish** that can grow to a length of about 10 ft. (3 m).

Left: The bony helmet and colored wattles make the **cassowary** look like a creature from another planet.

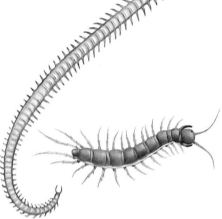

Below are two of the many kinds of **centipedes**. The longer species has from 77 to 83 pairs of legs; the other 15 pairs.

Cavefish   N, V, E

The name of 32 species of fish that are largely unrelated to one another, but which all share features resulting from a life spent in darkness. All lack skin pigment so that they are pink in color due to the blood showing through their skin. Most are quite blind, though in many cases the young fish start out with fully developed eyes which disappear as they mature.

Centipede

Any of about 3,000 many-legged ARTHROPODS. Most centipedes have between 15 and 23 pairs of legs, one pair for each body segment, but one European centipede has up to 177 pairs. Centipedes vary in length from .8 in. (2 cm) to the 10.6 in. (27 cm) of a species which lives in the tropical rain forests of the Americas and has 23 pairs of legs. Because centipedes do not have a waterproof body covering, to prevent them from drying out they have to live in damp surroundings. They are active predators, hunting insects, spiders, worms, and other small animals. The front pair of legs act as poisonous claws and are used for paralyzing and killing their prey. Many centipedes can run surprisingly quickly to capture their prey.

CLASS: Chilopoda

Chaffinch

One of the most common of all European birds, the chaffinch is found throughout the continent, and large flocks migrate annually to North Africa and the Middle East. Like all FINCHES, chaffinches have stout bills for cracking seeds. They also eat insects, spiders, and earthworms. Outside the breeding season, chaffinches form flocks several dozen strong which are often segregated by sex and can often be seen with other small species. The females build a nest of grass, roots, and moss.

ORDER: Passeriformes
FAMILY: Fringillidae
SPECIES: *Fringilla coelebs*

Chalcid wasp

The chalcid wasps, of which there are thousands of species, are only distantly related to the true wasps and are mostly very small insects. Few are more than about 0.1 in. (2.5 mm) long, and the group actually contains the smallest of all insects – the fairy flies. These tiny creatures, some of them only .01 in. (.25 mm) long, grow up inside the eggs of other insects. Most of the larger chalcids are also parasites of other insects. Eggs are often laid in the caterpillars and *chrysalises* of butterflies and moths, and large numbers of chalcid grubs grow up inside these hosts and kill them. Many chalcid wasps have beautiful metallic colors.

ORDER: Hymenoptera

Chameleon   N, V

There are about 80 species of these slow-moving lizards. Some are less than 2 in. (5 cm) long, while others grow to 24 in. (60 cm). Most live in forests in Africa south of the Sahara Desert. The common chameleon ranges from the Middle East along the coast of North Africa to southern Spain.

Chameleons are probably the strangest of all lizards. Each has a high body, flattened from side to side. Jackson's chameleon has horns, and the flap-necked chameleon has a "helmet." Many species wrap their tails around a twig for extra grip. The toes of each foot are joined so as to produce feet like tongs, which give them a firm hold on the branches. The chameleons are slow-moving animals, rarely moving more than one leg at a time, and anchoring it firmly before moving the next. Their eyes move constantly in search of food

A male **chaffinch** in flight clearly shows its characteristic double white wing bands.

or danger, each eye swiveling independently of the other. If a chameleon sees an insect or some other prey within range, it shoots out a tongue longer than its own body length. The victim is trapped on the sticky tongue tip and whipped back to the mouth, the whole attack being over in a second.

Chameleons can change color in response to changes in light, temperature, or emotional state. Color change may act as camouflage or as an indication of mood to other chameleons; for example, an angry chameleon turns black.

Some chameleons lay eggs, others bear live young. Within a day the young are catching prey.

ORDER: Squamata
FAMILY: Chamaeleontidae

Chamois   R

The chamois is a species of GOAT ANTELOPE. It stands about 30 in. (80 cm) at the shoulder and weighs up to 88 lb. (40 kg). Both sexes have horns, which can grow to 10 in. (25 cm) long. The coat is long, with a thick under-fur, tawny in summer and dark brown to black in winter. There is a dark line down the middle of the back. Most chamois live in alpine forests around the *tree line*. Some reach the *snow line* in summer, but they move down in winter. The chamois is found in southern Europe, Asia Minor, and the Caucasus region. When alarmed, this agile animal can make tremendous leaps across ravines and up almost sheer rock faces. It is also noted for its excellent sight and hearing. Its enemies are wolves and lynx.

ORDER: Artiodactyla
FAMILY: Bovidae
SPECIES: *Rupicapra rupicapra*

The **chameleon** is noted for three things: it can change color to suit its surroundings or its mood; it can move its eyes independently of each other; and it has a tongue that shoots out at lightning speed to a length greater than that of the animal's body.

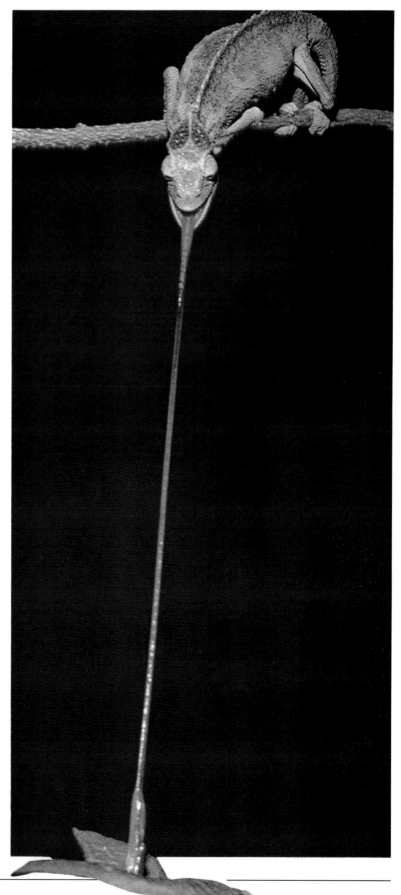

Char N, R

Fish that are close relatives of SALMON and TROUT, which they greatly resemble. European char either spend their whole lives in lakes and streams, or else live mostly at sea, particularly in the Arctic Ocean. They return to inland waters only to breed.
ORDER: Salmoniformes
FAMILY: Salmonidae

Characin N, V

A family of tropical freshwater fish well known to people who keep aquariums. Very familiar examples include the brilliant little TETRAS and the swordtail characin, another member of the same genus. Other well-known characins include the freshwater HATCHETFISH and the dreaded PIRANHA of the rivers of Central and South America. Most characins live either in these rivers or in those of tropical Africa.

However, this huge family, which is often subdivided into as many as 30 subfamilies, contains a host of other, less well-known fish. They range in size from just over 1.2 in. (3 cm) to 5 ft. (1.5 m), and vary greatly in appearance. An outstanding feature of characins as a whole is the way in which they imitate fish of other families. For example, one looks like a TROUT, another looks like a MULLET, a third resembles a HERRING, and so on. Most characins have the general appearance of MINNOWS and CARP.

Examples of carnivores, omnivores, and plant-eaters can be found among the characins. Spawning and egg laying in general resemble those of many other freshwater fish, although one member of the family, the spraying characin, has the curious habit of spraying its eggs onto land, where they develop with less risk of being eaten.
ORDER: Cypriniformes
FAMILY: Characidae

Cheetah V

The cheetah is the fastest animal on land. Compared with the LION or LEOPARD, the cheetah's legs are extremely long and the head is small. Head and body combined measure about 4 ft. (1.2 m) and

The Congo tetra is one of the few **characins** from Africa.

the tail is half as long again. It stands about 1 yard (1 m) high and weighs over 100 lb. (45 kg). Closely spaced black spots cover most of the body, which is tawny or gray with white underparts. Unlike other cats, the cheetah has blunt claws that can be only partly retracted. Cheetahs live in open countryside in Africa and southwest Asia. In India they are now thought to be extinct.

The cheetah's body gives a general impression of a lithe and speedy creature and it can certainly run very fast over short distances. Someone reportedly timed a cheetah running at 70 mph (114 km/h) over a distance of 700 yards (640 m). But many people accept a likelier top speed of about 60 mph (97 km/h). Sprinting helps the cheetah catch its prey. Unlike other cats, who stalk their prey slowly or lie in wait and pounce, cheetahs walk toward their prey, and then speed up to a sprint. In this way they run down antelopes, ostriches, and hares. But if the chase proves long, the cheetah gives up, exhausted by its sudden burst of speed.

Breeding is thought to take place at any time of the year, and litters contain 2 to 5 cubs. Studies in east Africa suggest that half of the young die in the first year of life.
ORDER: Carnivora
FAMILY: Felidae
SPECIES: *Acinonyx jubatus*

Chicken

Although strictly defined as any young bird, this word is normally used for the domestic fowl – probably the most common bird in the world. It was domesticated at least 4,000 years ago and is thought to have been bred from the red jungle fowl of India and Southeast Asia. It was first used for religious and sacrificial purposes, the eggs and flesh not being used until much later. There are now dozens of commerical breeds as well as ornamental ones bred for their attractive plumage. Like most game birds, the chicken is a vegetarian, eating mostly seeds, fruits, and leaves. It has a strong *gizzard* in which the seeds are ground up with the aid of small stones which the bird swallows. The bird also enjoys worms and insects. The wings are short and can sustain only short bursts of flight. Roosters can be recognized by the larger wattles and combs on the head and also by the glossy greenish tail feathers.

ORDER: Galliformes
FAMILY: Phasianidae

Chimaera

A type of fish which in many ways comes between the bony fish and the sharklike fish. Like bony fish, chimaeras have a gill cover protecting the gills. Details of their food canal and their upper jaw are also like those of bony fish. But like sharks, chimaeras have a skeleton made of cartilage and not of bone. Their eggs are horny capsules like those of many sharks, and the male chimaera, like the male shark, has two claspers which he uses to impregnate the female during mating.

A **chimpanzee** can communicate emotions by changing its expression. This one is showing great attention.

A young **chimpanzee** with a parent.

Chimaeras are strange-looking fish – their name means "fabulous monster" – with a large head and eyes and a body tapering to an insignificant tail fin. The snout can be rounded, pointed, trunklike, or plowlike, depending on the species. The teeth may be large and rabbitlike, for cracking the shells of mollusks and crustaceans. Many chimaeras have a poisonous spine at the front of their *dorsal fin*. They can be large fish, up to 5 ft. (1.5 m) long.

ORDER: Chimaeriformes

Chimpanzee   V

The chimpanzee is one of the great apes. Because it is nearest in intelligence to humans, it is one of the most studied and popular of animals. Chimpanzees are the best tool-makers apart from humans – they can use sticks to extract honey, ants, and termites from nests; and stones to crack nuts, or as missiles. They chew up leaves and make them into a sponge, which is then used to extract water from a hollow in a tree.

Chimpanzees live in tropical rain forests of Africa, ranging from the Niger basin to Angola. At night, they sleep in nests made of branches and vines in the trees. They often search for food on the ground. They usually walk on all fours, although they sometimes run on three legs, leaving one free to hold food. They can walk upright, with their toes turned outward, standing 3 to 5 ft. (90 to 152 cm) high. Their hair is long, coarse, and black, except for a white patch near the rump. The face, ears, hands, and feet are free of hair.

Chimpanzees live in groups of up to 40 but they often wander away from the troop on their own. Within a group, males are arranged in a social order, the inferior ones respecting the superior ones. The members of a group spend much time grooming themselves or others. Seven hours a day may be spent on feeding. Fruit, leaves, and roots are the main foods, although it has been found that some chimpanzees like meat. They have been seen catching young BUSHBUCKS, BUSH PIGS, COLOBUS MONKEYS, and BABOONS.

The *gestation period* is about 230 days and the young depend entirely on their mothers for two years. Young chimpanzees are playful and friendly, but they may become ill-tempered in old age.
ORDER: Primates
FAMILY: Pongidae
SPECIES: *Pan troglodytes*

Chinchilla

The chinchilla looks like a small rabbit with a squirrel's tail and is related to the VISCACHAS, AGOUTIS, and GUINEA PIGS. Chinchillas once thrived all over the Andes Mountains of South America. Valued for their soft fur, they were hunted so much that wild chinchillas are now found only in the high mountains of northern Chile. Chinchillas live in colonies in burrows among rocks. They come out at night and eat grasses and herbs.
ORDER: Rodentia
FAMILY: Chinchillidae
SPECIES: *Chinchilla laniger*

In the year 1899, half a million **chinchilla** pelts were exported from Chile.

The western **chipmunk** above stores food in the fall and sleeps much of the winter.

Chinese water deer

The Chinese water deer of China and Korea stands 18 to 22 in. (44 to 55 cm) at the shoulder and is about 3 ft. (90 cm) long. It weighs up to 36 lb. (16 kg). This small animal is unique among deer as it can give birth to up to 7 fawns, although 4 or 5 is usual. The coat is a light yellowish-brown to pale reddish-brown in summer, turning dark brown in winter. There is little difference between the sexes. The males have no antlers, but their upper canine teeth are long and tusklike. They are used in fights between males in the breeding season. This deer lives in swampy areas in its natural home, but has become adapted to woodland life where it has escaped from captivity.
ORDER: Artiodactyla
FAMILY: Cervidae
SPECIES: *Hydropotes inermis*

Chipmunk   N, E

Chipmunks are common GROUND SQUIRRELS. There are about 20 kinds. The eastern chipmunk lives in the eastern United States and Canada. The slightly smaller western chipmunk is found throughout North America and northern Asia. The chipmunk's fur is reddish-brown with dark stripes on the back. The tail is not as bushy as that of tree squirrels.

Chipmunks live in burrow systems underground, usually in pasture land or open woodland. Their main foods are berries, fruits, nuts, and seeds, but they also eat slugs, snails, and small insects. Food not immediately needed is carried in cheek pouches and stored away for the winter.
ORDER: Rodentia
FAMILY: Sciuridae

Chiton

Chitons are a very old group of MOLLUSKS of which there are 700 species. They are flat and oval in shape, and cling to the undersides of seashore rocks. The chiton's shell is made up of eight plates, and the lower part of the body consists of a muscular foot, similar to that of a SNAIL. There are no eyes on the animal's head, but some species have eyes on the plates of the shell, sometimes as many as 11,500. Most chitons are small but one species that lives on the west coast of North America grows up to 13 in. (33 cm) long. Chitons feed on algae which they scrape off rocks.
CLASS: Amphineura
ORDER: Chitonida

The **chiton** is one of the most primitive of mollusks.

Chough

The name given to two species belonging to the CROW family, the red-billed chough, and the alpine chough. Red-billed and Alpine choughs are found all over Europe and southern Asia. Red-billed choughs prefer sea cliffs, while the alpine chough lives inland and frequents mountain precipices. In the Himalayas they have been found breeding at 21,000 ft. (6,500 m). Choughs often behave

The **red-billed chough** has red legs and beak. Alpine choughs have a yellow beak.

as if they are enjoying themselves. They play elaborate games such as "follow the leader" and play in the air currents around cliff faces.
ORDER: Passeriformes
FAMILY: Corvidae
SPECIES: *Pyrrhocorax pyrrhocorax* (red-billed); *Pyrrhocorax graculus* (alpine)

Chub

The chub is a freshwater fish of North American and European rivers. It belongs to the CARP family. A fully grown European chub is about 24 in. (60 cm) long, with a broad head and powerful jaws with which it catches smaller fish. Anglers often catch chub, but usually throw the fish back in the river because the flesh has an uninteresting taste.
ORDER: Cypriniformes
FAMILY: Cyprinidae
SPECIES: *Leuciscus cephalus*

The European **chub**.

Chuckwalla

The chuckwalla is a plump North American LIZARD. Some individuals grow to 18 in. (46 cm) long and weigh 4.5 lb. (2 kg). They live in rocky deserts of the southwestern United States. Most lizards eat small animals, but wild chuckwallas eat the flowers of certain desert plants. If threatened by an enemy, a chuckwalla hides in the nearest rock crevice. It grips tightly with its toes and wedges itself firmly in by blowing up its body with air. In their hot desert homes, chuckwallas are active only from late March to early August, when food is abundant. They sleep for the rest of the year.
ORDER: Squamata
FAMILY: Iguanidae
SPECIES: *Sauromalus obesus*

Below: **Cicadas** spend most of their time in trees, sucking sap from beneath the bark.

Cicada   N, V

The cicadas are fairly large sap-sucking BUGS that feed mainly in the trees. Their long beaks easily penetrate the bark of the smaller branches to reach the sap beneath. The insects are difficult to see when sitting on the bark, but the males give away their presence by their incredibly shrill calls. These are produced by a small membrane on each side of the body.

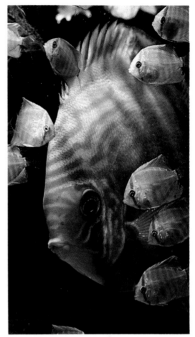

This **cichlid** is the discus. Like all cichlids, it takes good care of its young.

The membrane is vibrated very rapidly and it gives out a high-pitched, warbling whistle to attract the females. Eggs are laid in the soil, and the *nymphs* take sap from various roots. They have powerful front legs with which they dig their way through the soil. They remain under the ground for several years – 17 years for one American species – and come up only when it is time for the adult to break out of the nymphal skin. Most of the 1,500 or so species are tropical.
ORDER: Hemiptera-Homoptera
FAMILY: Cicadidae

Cichlid   N, R, V, E

A family of fish containing 600 species, many of which are favorite fish for tropical aquariums. Cichlids live in many rivers and lakes all over Africa and in Central and South America, southern India, and Sri Lanka. The freshwater ANGELFISH and many other cichlids have deep, narrow bodies with colors which are always brilliant. These colors brighten even further in the male fish when he is attracting a female or frightening off a rival. Many cichlids have elaborate courting rituals, involving mouth-to-mouth tugging contests between male and female, and digging and cleaning activities that mime nest building.

After egg laying and fertilization, both parent cichlids guard the nest. Later they may transport the eggs by mouth to nearby pits dug in the sand. Newly hatched cichlid *fry* are well looked after by their parents, who may take the fry into their mouths for protection.

ORDER: Perciformes
FAMILY: Cichlidae

Civet   N, R, E

Civets belong to the same family as the MONGOOSE and the GENET. They have a sharp muzzle and long body and tail. In habits and pattern of coat they resemble the small cats. The African civet lives in Africa south of the Sahara. The large Indian civet and the small Indian civet live in south and Southeast Asia. Civets are forest-dwelling animals, eating insects,

frogs, birds, and fruit. They climb and swim well, and capture some of their food in water. Some have been seen catching crabs on the seashore. There are usually 2 to 3 young in a litter, born in a hole in the ground or in dense cover. Man's interest in civets has been mainly to collect the *musk* from glands near the reproductive organs. The concentrated substance smells offensive to the human nose but is pleasant when diluted. It is sometimes used in perfumes.

ORDER: Carnivora
FAMILY: Viverridae

Clam   N, V

Clam is a name given to many bivalve MOLLUSKS and it has different meanings in different parts of the world. In the U.S. it is applied to any edible *bivalves*, such as the soft clam or the great clam. Elsewhere the term may apply only to freshwater MUSSELS. One species over which there is no

The tridacna is a large **clam** of tropical reefs.

dispute is the giant clam. These huge clams live in the shallow waters of the Indo-Pacific coral reefs, and can be more than 4.5 ft. (1.2 m) across and weigh up to 550 lb. (254 kg). The margins of the shell are corrugated in such a way that when the valves close they fit into each other. There have been many stories in the past of giant clams snapping shut on the leg of an unwary swimmer, trapping him until he drowns. In fact, this is most unlikely, as there are no such fatalities on record, and the clam probably closes its shell too slowly ever to trap anyone.

CLASS: Bivalvia
ORDER: Adapedonta

Clawed frog

The clawed frog is tongueless. Females are larger than the European common frog. Clawed frogs live in tropical and southern Africa, in swamps, streams, and ponds. They seldom leave the water, where they are powerful swimmers. Their front legs are short and weak, and each ends in four straight fingers. Back legs are long and muscular, with large

webs between the toes. Clawed frogs can change color from mottled to black or pale buff to match their background. They seize their prey between their front feet and their mouths. At breeding time a female lays up to 2,000 eggs.

ORDER: Anura
FAMILY: Pipidae
SPECIES: *Xenopus laevis*

The **click beetle** and its larva. The larva does damage to potatoes and cereal roots.

Click beetle   N, V, E

The click beetles are small, slender insects. They are able to right themselves when they fall onto their backs. They flick themselves into the air and turn over before they fall back to the ground. This action is accompanied by a loud click, from which they get their name. Some of the species have bright, metallic colors, but most are dull brown. Adult beetles chew pollen and lap nectar from flowers, but the *larvae*, known as wireworms, feed on plant roots and do much damage to crops.

ORDER: Coleoptera
FAMILY: Elateridae

Climbing perch

The climbing perch is a freshwater fish of Southeast Asia. It is about 9 in. (23 cm) long and grayish-green in color. This small fish is

The **clawed frog**, *Xenopus*, from South Africa can change its color pattern to match its surroundings.

famous because it leaves its home pond when this is beginning to dry up, and travels overland for considerable distances to find another pond.

The fish "walks" overland with the aid of spines on its gill covers which dig into the soil, so giving it purchase. It is also aided in walking by its *pectoral fins* and tail. In order to leave the water it has had to make a remarkable adaptation. A rosettelike development of the gills, richly supplied with blood vessels, acts like a lung, enabling the fish to breathe air directly and so to survive for long periods out of water.

ORDER: Perciformes
FAMILY: Anabantidae
SPECIES: *Anabas testudineus*

Clothes moth

The name clothes moth is given to several species of small moths whose *larvae* feed on wool and other animal materials. They will feed on carpets and other furnishings, as well as on clothes, if undisturbed. They do not feed on vegetable or synthetic fibers. The adult moths are no more than .4 in. (1 cm) long and their wings are brown- or silvery-gray, with fringe around the edges. They are secretive insects, rarely flying and preferring to scuttle away into a crevice. The larva of the case-bearing clothes moth builds a tube of silk and fiber around itself and carries it around. The original home of the clothes moths must have been in birds' nests and similar places, where the grubs ate fur and feathers.

ORDER: Lepidoptera
FAMILY: Tineidae

The **clothes moth's** larva chews holes in anything woolen.

Coalfish

The coalfish is a marine food fish of European waters, a close relative of the COD. It grows up to a length of about a 1 yard (1 m) and has a silvery-dark body with three *dorsal fins* and two *anal fins*. The *pelvic fins* are just behind the gill covers. Like the cod, the coalfish has a short *barbel,* or feeler, on the lower lip.

The main spawning grounds of the coalfish are the Norwegian and British coasts, although the full range of the coalfish extends from the Arctic to the Mediterranean. Schools of coalfish are inclined to feed on the *fry* of their larger relative the cod, but coalfish also eat many other kinds of small fish and shellfish. The coalfish also has other names. In Europe it was

A **coati** will poke his long nose into anything that promises food.

once known as the saithe. In the United States it is called the pollack.

ORDER: Gadiformes
FAMILY: Gadidae
SPECIES: *Gadus virens*

Coati

The coatis are related to the RACCOON. They are up to 4.5 ft. (1.4 m) long, of which 2.4 ft. (.75 m) is a striped tail which is generally held vertically with the

When frightened, the **cobra** rears up and spreads its hood.

tip curled over. They have small ears and a flat forehead, which runs down to a long, mobile snout that extends beyond the jaw. The general color is reddish-brown to black, with yellowish underparts, and black and gray face markings. The two main species are the ring-tailed coati which inhabits the northern parts of South America, and the brown coati, which lives in Central America and is occasionally seen in the southern United States.

Male coatis are solitary, but the females and young live in bands of up to 20. They travel through the forest foraging for fruit and small animals. Breeding takes place in the dry season, when each band is joined by a male. The young are born in a nest in a tree.

ORDER: Carnivora
FAMILY: Procyonidae
SPECIES: *Nasua nasua* (ring-tailed); *Nasua narica* (brown)

Cobra   N, E

Various species of true cobra live in Africa and Asia. They include the Indian cobra and the Egyptian cobra. Most cobras are medium-sized snakes, about 2 yd. (2 m) long. When frightened or excited they rear up, and movable ribs spread the skin behind the neck until it forms a flattish hood. Anyone who comes too near is likely to be bitten, and cobra venom is extremely poisonous. Victims suffer bleeding and swelling. But the venom's chief ingredients are nerve poisons that paralyze the nervous system. Victims of the Indian cobra may die of heart failure and breathing failure in only 15 minutes. Many experts believe the Indian cobra to be one of the most dangerous of all snakes. In India alone it kills about 10,000 people every year. Some cobras attack by spitting venom directly at the eyes of the victim. If their venom gets into the eyes it causes blindness for a time.

Cobras mainly eat rodents. Many accidents happen when the snakes enter homes in search of rats. Frogs, toads, and birds are also eaten. Cobras climb trees to plunder nests. The Egyptian cobra will raid poultry runs. The Cape cobra often eats snakes, and the black-and-white cobra is said to hunt fish.

MONGOOSES and GENETS are among the cobra's enemies. But in a fight the cobra sometimes wins. Its inflated hood may help protect the neck from bites. Cobras also play dead, going limp until danger passes.

ORDER: Squamata
FAMILY: Elapidae
SPECIES: *Naja naja* (India); *Naja haje (Egyptian)*

Cockatoo N, V, E

The cockatoos are a group of 16 species of the PARROT family. They include the cockatiels, gang-gangs, and galahs. Cockatoos look like parrots, but have crests which they can raise at will. Most are white, sometimes with pink or yellow tinges, and colored crests, but some are black or gray.

A pink **cockatoo** from Australia displays its erect crest.

Cockatoos are found in the Australasian region, ranging from the Celebes in the west to the Solomon Islands in the east. They generally live in wooded country, though some extend to woodland borders and open scrub. Cockatoos are mainly vegetarian, eating seeds, fruits, and nuts. Some are pests and raid cereal crops, trampling down the plants and taking the seeds. Others attack fruit trees. Cockatoos make good pet birds, being able to mimic human and other sounds.

ORDER: Psittaciformes
FAMILY: Psittacidae

Cockchafer

Also known as the May bug, the cockchafer is a bulky brown beetle about 1 in. (25 mm) long. Its pointed hind end is black and sticks out beyond the *elytra*. It flies noisily in May and June and often crashes into lit windows at night. The insect is a serious pest in both adult and larval stages. The adults strip the leaves from a wide variety of trees, while the fat white grubs live under the ground and do serious damage to the roots of cereal and other crops, as well as trees. The cockchafer is widely distributed in Europe and Asia, and several similar species live in other parts of the world.

ORDER: Coleoptera
FAMILY: Scarabaeidae
SPECIES: *Melolontha melolontha*

Cockchafer and larva

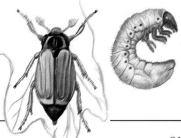

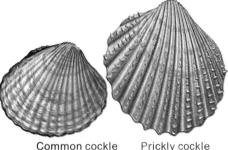

Common cockle   Prickly cockle

Cockle

Cockle is the name given to about 200 species of *bivalve* MOLLUSKS. They have unusually rounded, ribbed shells and are found from high-tide level down to 8,000 ft. (2,400 m) deep in the sea. Most cockles live embedded in the sand or mud of the seabed, with a pair of short tubes, or *siphons*, projecting above the surface. The cockle draws water in through one tube and ejects it through the other, filtering food and oxygen from it as it passes over the gills. The eyes are on tentacles on the siphons.
CLASS: Bivalvia
ORDER: Heterodonta

Cock-of-the-rock

The two species of cock-of-the-rock are ornate but uncommon South American birds belonging to the same family as the COTINGA. They are noted for their variety of crests and *wattles*. Cocks-of-the-rock live in the dense, damp forests around the Amazon basin. They are mainly fruit-eaters, but also feed on insects and snails. The males have elaborate displays.
ORDER: Passeriformes
FAMILY: Cotingidae

The **collared dove** has a black stripe edged with white on the back of its neck.

Cockroach

The cockroaches are flattened, greasy insects with long, spiky legs and very long *antennae*. Their bodies reach 3 in. (8 cm) or more in length, although most species are much smaller. Many can fly well, but others are wingless or have very short wings. When present, the front wings are rather leathery and they protect the more delicate hind wings. Cockroaches are scavenging insects and most of them live in the tropics. They come out at night to feed on dead animals and fallen fruit. A few of the 4,000 or so species live wild in Europe, but the most familiar species are the "domestic" cockroaches – tropical species which have become established in heated buildings. The American cockroach is a typical example of this. Cockroaches lay their eggs in little "purses," which the females carry around with them for a time. The youngsters grow up without a pupal stage.
ORDER: Dictyoptera

Cod

The cod is second only in importance to the HERRING as a food fish. The Atlantic cod is a large fish, up to 2 yd. (2 m) long and weighing as much as 200 lb. (96 kg), although the fish people eat are much smaller. The cod has a plump, olive-green or brown body, patterned with spots, and a silvery belly. On its lower lip it has a prominent *barbel*, or feeler. Most cod are trawled at depths of 65 to 650 ft. (20 to 200 m), where they feed on smaller fish and sometimes SQUID. A female cod lays as many as six million eggs each year, but the vast majority get eaten by other fish. Those tiny young, or *fry*, that do survive sometimes get protection by living between the stinging tentacles of JELLYFISH.
ORDER: Gadiformes
FAMILY: Gadidae
SPECIES: *Gadus morhua*

Coelacanth   v

The coelacanth is a living fossil, perhaps the most famous fish of this century. It belongs to a large order of fish that were thought to have become extinct 70 million years ago, and is apparently its sole survivor. It is important to zoologists because the coelacanth and its extinct relatives belong to a larger group of fish, the lobefins, from which the first land animals arose.

The first coelacanth to be identified was caught off the South African coast by a trawler in 1938. Unlike any coelacanth that had previously been caught, this one was seen by a zoologist, who recognized the large blue fish for what it was. Many more coelacanths have since been caught.

The living coelacanth is a large, deep-water fish with a heavy body weighing about 110 lb. (50 kg). Its body, about 5 ft. (1.5 m) long, is blue in color and is covered with scales which, unusually for a bony fish, have many small toothlike points. In some ways, these scales are more like those of nonbony fish such as sharks.
CLASS: Sarcopterygii
ORDER: Crossopterygii
FAMILY: Latimeriidae
SPECIES: *Latimeria chalumnae*

Collared dove

A dove measuring 11 in. (28 cm) in length. It is distinguished by the narrow black collar around the back of the neck. Collared doves are birds of farmland and gardens, and can be seen in city centers. They feed mainly on seeds. Collared doves are found in Africa, Asia, and Europe. Before 1930, they were confined to southeastern Europe and then began a remarkable expansion to the northwest. They are now found throughout central Europe and extend to Britain, Ireland, and Scandinavia, while some have bred in Iceland.
ORDER: Columbiformes
FAMILY: Columbidae
SPECIES: *Streptopelia decaocto*

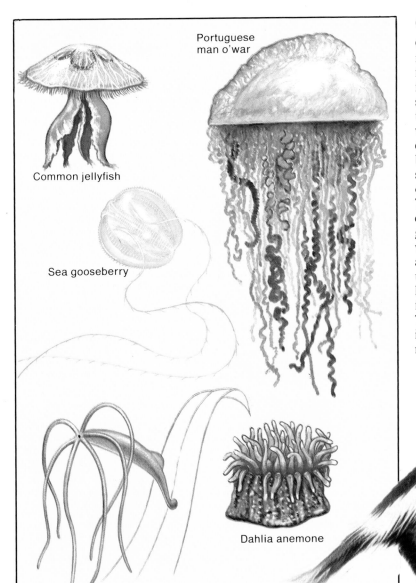

Common jellyfish

Portuguese man o'war

Sea gooseberry

Dahlia anemone

Brown hydra

Coelenterates

This animal phylum contains more than 10,000 species of aquatic animals. They include CORALS, SEA ANEMONES, and JELLYFISH, as well as the well-known HYDRA of ponds and streams. The soft body is little more than a bag with walls consisting of two layers of muscular cells separated by a layer of jelly. There is only one opening, which is surrounded by a number of arms, or tentacles. These normally bear stinging cells with which the coelenterates catch their prey. There is no brain, but a network of nerves controls the actions of the tentacles and ensures that they push in the right direction. New individuals, known as *polyps*, grow from buds on the parent, but they do not always separate completely and they later produce buds themselves. A branching colonly thus builds up. The CORALS are the best known of these branching forms.

Colobus monkey R, E

Colobus monkeys are shy animals, rarely coming out of the dense forest where they live. They range from Senegal to Ethiopia and southward to Angola, but despite this range, they are common nowhere. Of the three species, the endangered black colobus is the best known. Its coat usually has short, black fur with long plumes of white on the tail and sides. There is also white on the chin, cheeks, and forehead. The endangered red colobus has a black body with chestnut-colored head, arms, and legs. The rare olive colobus is unusual in that the mother carries her new-born young in her mouth for the first few weeks of its life. This is probably because her hair is too short for it to grip. Colobus monkeys live in family groups.

The **colobus monkey** can make enormous leaps from tree to tree.

They are mainly leaf-eaters. Their chief enemies are eagles and man.
ORDER: Primates
FAMILY: Colobidae
SPECIES: *Colobus polykomos* (black); *Colobus badius* (red); *Colobus verus* (olive)

Colorado beetle

The Colorado beetle is a serious pest of potatoes. It is one of a large

The **colorado beetle** is a dangerous pest. It has been the cause of famine because of chewing potato leaves.

family of beetles known as LEAF BEETLES. Both the adult, easily recognized by its black and yellow stripes, and the bright pink grub feed avidly on the leaves and stems of the potato plant. Whole plants may be nibbled to the ground, so no tubers can develop. Adult beetles hibernate in the soil and emerge to lay eggs in spring. The beetle is a native of North America, but found its way to Europe in the 1920s.

ORDER: Coleoptera
FAMILY: Chrysomelidae
SPECIES: *Leptinotarsa decemlineata*

Conch

A family of large sea snails, whose shells have been used as trumpets. The shells have a long, narrow opening and an outer lip which is expanded to form a broad plate. Conches range in size from .5 to 24 in. (14 mm to 60 cm), the largest being the queen conch. They have two large eyes, carried on stalks on either side of a stout *proboscis*. Most conches live in warm, shallow tropical waters where they feed on seaweed. At rest they tend to bury themselves in sand or gravel. Conches leap over the seabed by means of their large foot which has a sharp-edged *operculum* on the hind end. The conch uses this operculum to push itself along and as a weapon.

CLASS: Gastropoda
ORDER: Mesogastropoda
FAMILY: Strombidae

Condor   N, E

The condor is the world's largest flying bird, with a wingspan of 10 ft. (3 m) and weighing up to 24 lb. (11 kg). Of the two species, the Andean condor is still fairly common, but the Californian condor is almost extinct. Only about sixty birds survive. Hunters have found the large target of the condor irresistible and the condor's slow breeding rate handicaps its chances of survival. It lays one egg every other year.

Condors look like VULTURES, with the same naked heads and necks, and are mainly scavengers, feeding on carrion. But they are not related to the true vultures of the Old World. Condors are superb fliers, soaring to great heights on the thermal air currents over mountains. They have excellent eyesight and can spot a carcass at a great distance. If one condor suddenly drops toward the ground, other condors know it has found food and quickly fly to the feast. Apart from carrion, condors will also eat live prey, such as lambs, young llamas, and deer. Near coasts they will eat dead fish and seals, as well as shellfish.

ORDER: Falconiformes
FAMILY: Cathartidae
SPECIES: *Vultur gryphus* (Andean); *Gymnogyps californianus* (Californian)

Cone shell

There are between 500 and 600 species of sea snails in the family Conidae, and they are known as cone shells from the shape of their shells. They range in size from very small up to about 9 in. (23 cm) long. They live in the shallow

The queen **conch** shell can be as much as 24 in. (60 cm) long. Conches have been used as trumpets from the earliest times. The Triton shell of Greek mythology was a conch.

The Andean **condor** is the world's largest flying bird. It can reach heights of over 2.5 mi. (4,000 m), gliding upward on rising air currents.

tropical and subtropical waters of the Atlantic and Indian Oceans, and around the East Indies. Cone shells are carnivorous, eating worms, mollusks or small fish. They have hollow teeth through which they inject poison into their victims. The sting of some of the large species can kill a man.

CLASS: Gastropoda
ORDER: Neogastropoda
FAMILY: Conidae

Conger

The conger, or conger EEL, is a large marine eel which grows up to 10 ft. (3 m) long and weighs up to 100 lb. (45 kg). It has a light to dark brown scaleless body with large, sharp eyes, strong jaws, and sharp teeth, showing that it is a predator. One story says that a conger bit off the heel of a fisherman's boot!

Like the related freshwater EEL, the conger spawns only once, then dies. Also like its smaller relative, it begins life as a tiny, leaflike fish which makes long migrations at sea, gradually changing in form to resemble the adult eel.

ORDER: Anguilliformes
FAMILY: Congridae
SPECIES: *Conger conger*

Coot   N, R

The ten species of coots belong to the RAIL family and are closely related to the MOORHEN. They are

found all over the world. Coots are dark-colored water birds. Most species are distinguished by the white shield that lies above the bill. On each toe, coots have lobed flaps that open to act like paddles. These leave the toes free to move, so that coots are nimble on land,

unlike birds with webbed feet. Coots are to be found on fairly large bodies of water, gathering in flocks outside the breeding season. They nest among tall water plants at the edges of lakes.

ORDER: Gruiformes
FAMILY: Rallidae

The **conger** can grow to a length of 10 ft. (3 m).

Red-knobbed **coots** among water flowers at the margin of a lake in Kenya.

Small copper

Small copper caterpillar

Purple-shot copper male

Copper butterfly   N, V, E

The copper butterflies are quite small, fast-flying butterflies whose wings have the color and luster of polished copper on the upper surface. Many are marked with black spots and streaks, and several have a blue or purple sheen as well. They are related to the BLUE BUTTERFLIES and are widely distributed in the cooler parts of the Northern Hemisphere. There are many species, of which the small copper, also known as the American copper, is the most familiar. The butterflies frequent flowery places and often defend a particular clump of flowers against other butterflies by darting out at newcomers as they approach. The caterpillars of the coppers are somewhat sluglike in shape and almost all feed on docks and related plants.
ORDER: Lepidoptera
FAMILY: Lycaenidae

Coral

Coral belong to the class of sea creatures often called "flower-animals." They are similar to SEA ANEMONES except that they are surrounded and supported by a hard, chalky skeleton. True coral, often called stony coral, may be solitary or live in colonies. A solitary polyp lives in a chalk cup or on a mushroom-shaped chalky skeleton. The *polyps* of a colony-living coral unite in thousands to form a sheet of tissue covering the chalky skeleton. Although the skeleton is often white when dead, when the coral is alive and covered with a continuous layer of flesh it can be beautifully colored and form a variety of shapes.

Most coral live in tropical seas. Only a few species thrive in temperate or polar regions. Reef-building coral form huge reefs along thousands of miles of tropical and subtropical shores, especially in the Indian Ocean. These coral grow only in very clear water and are absent from areas where large rivers flow into the sea. Coral feed by catching small swimming animals in their tentacles. Tiny single-celled plants live in the tissues of reef coral, and produce chemicals which help the polyps to make their lime skeletons. Coral reproduce in two ways: either sexually by producing eggs and sperm cells, or asexually by budding.

A living **coral** colony; the individual polyps that make it up are only .4 in. (10 mm) in diameter.

Soft coral are not true coral. They are usually treelike, the centers of the stems and branches being strengthened by a chalky substance, colored red or black. The polyps have eight tentacles, whereas those of true coral have six, or multiples of six.
CLASS: Anthozoa

Coral snake

True coral snakes live in Asia and the Americas. They include two species found in North America: the common coral snake which lives in Mexico and the southeastern United States, and the Arizona coral snake, which lives in Mexico and the southwestern United States. The Arizona coral snake is shorter than the common coral snake, which measures about 1 yd. (1 m) when fully grown.

The jaws of coral snakes do not open wide, so they eat only slender prey such as lizards and other snakes. The common coral snake lays 3 to 14 soft, slim eggs in May

or June which take about 11 weeks to hatch. The young measure about 7 in. (18 cm) long.

Coral snakes are slender, with a pattern of colored rings running around the body and tail. In both North American species the rings occur in the same order: black, yellow or white, and red. These brightly colored rings make coral snakes among the most gaudy of animals. They resemble the warning colors of creatures such as wasps and fire salamanders. All these animals are poisonous. True coral snakes are close relatives of the COBRAS, and are very poisonous, although they are not very aggressive.

ORDER: Squamata
FAMILY: Elapidae
SPECIES: *Micrurus fulvius* (common); *Micruroides euryxanthus* (Arizona)

Cormorant N, R

There are 30 species of cormorants. They are found all over the world except for the central Pacific region. Their webbed feet, upright stance, and long necks suggest that they lead an aquatic life. But they rarely fly far out to sea. Most are found along coasts or on inland waters.

The common cormorant is the

The **cormorant** is an expert fish-catcher. It can stay under water for more than a minute.

Continental form

Atlantic form

most widespread and largest of the species, being 40 in. (100 cm) long. It is also known as the great cormorant in North America, and the black cormorant in New Zealand. The plumage of the adult bird is generally glossy black with a white patch on the chin and cheeks. The green cormorant, called the shag in Britain, has a glossy, bottle-green plumage. Cormorants are expert divers and swimmers, and feed mainly on fish. In northeastern Asia, the Japanese cormorant is trained for fishing. A metal ring is placed around the bird's neck to prevent it from swallowing the catch.

ORDER: Pelecaniformes
FAMILY: Phalacrocoracidae
SPECIES: *Phalacrocorax carbo* (common)

The **corncrake** advertises its presence by the monotonous two-beat creaking call of the male, which is kept up for hours on end.

Corncrake R

The corncrake breeds in the fields and grasslands of Europe and Asia, and migrates to southern Africa and Asia. It hides in the grass, feeding on insects and other small animals, and depends on its streaky, light-brown plumage for camouflage. The spread of agriculture originally helped the corncrake to expand, as it is a bird of grassland, but the introduction of mowing machines has harmed the birds.

ORDER: Gruiformes
FAMILY: Rallidae
SPECIES: *Crex crex*

Cotinga N, V

A group of birds found mainly in the dense forests of the Amazon basin. There are about 90 species and many of the males have ornate plumage as well as crests and *wattles*. The COCK-OF-THE-ROCK is the most ornate, together with the umbrella bird. Cotingas are best known for their constant calling – the BELLBIRDS are especially notable in this respect. Many cotingas are fruit-eaters, but some also eat insects. Males often have elaborate courtship displays.

ORDER: Passeriformes
FAMILY: Cotingidae

Cottontail N, E, Ex

The cottontails are small RABBITS found throughout North and South America. The tail, brown above and white below, looks like a cotton ball and gives rise to the rabbit's name. The cottontail has shorter ears than the European rabbit, but its way of life is much the same.

There are about 13 species of cottontail, living in a range of habitats from woodland to desert. They feed on grass, and damage crops and young trees by nibbling and trampling them. The cottontail has many enemies, including fox, skunks, owls, hawks, and snakes. Its only defenses are to crouch motionless or, if seen, to run for its life. Like all rabbits, cottontails breed almost continuously and can have as many as five litters a year. The young are born in a hollow in the ground rather than in a burrow, and are blind for about ten days.

ORDER: Lagomorpha
FAMILY: Leporidae

Courser

Coursers are long-legged, plover-like shore birds. There are nine species, the most familiar being the cream-colored courser. It is a pale sandy color, with creamy legs, distinctive black primary wing feathers and a broad, black-and-

Courtship and mating

After an animal has found enough food for its own survival, its next need is to find a mate which will ensure the survival of its species. For animals that roam together in

The magnificent male Prince Rudolph's **bird of paradise** woos the dull-colored female by showing off its plumage and by strutting around.

herds, such as BISON, finding a possible mate is no problem. For species that lead solitary lives, finding another member of the same species may not be so easy.

Smell is one of the ways which help lone species to find a mate. Female moths, for example, release a faint perfume into the air, which will lure males from distances of over a half mile (1 km). We cannot smell the scent, but to another moth it is so attractive and powerful that not even the smell of rotting eggs can mask it. In the same way, female fish release into the water a chemical substance that can be detected by males of their species.

GLOWWORMS and FIREFLIES attract males by glowing brightly during the mating season. CRICKETS and GRASS-HOPPERS use sound to attract mates, but this time it is the male that attracts the female.

Once a mate has been found the ritual of courtship can begin. The courtship behavior of many animals is remarkably similar to that of humans – males display their courage and handsome features and even present the females with gifts. A male PENGUIN rolls a stone toward a female he is wooing. JACKDAWS and other birds bring gifts of food or nesting material. A male HERON starts to build a nest before he woos the female of his choice. The BOWER BIRD goes a stage further and constructs an elaborate tentlike structure, which he decorates with berries, flowers and, if he can get them, bits of glass and jewelry!

The main aspect of bird courtship, however, is display. The male bird struts in front of his chosen partner. In most cases he is much more brightly colored than the hen bird and he uses his color to the full in his courtship. One of the most beautiful displays is that of the PEACOCK, which spreads out its elaborate feathers like a huge fan. With this display go various ritual dances, which differ from species to species. Many distinctive courtship songs also help to make the female more receptive to the male's advances. If the male and female birds are alike, like GREBES, both may dance.

Among mammals, courtship tends to be less showy. Males are more likely to fight for the favors of the females or for the right to control a large harem. During the rutting season DEER make loud barking noises and two stags contest for superiority by a series of head-to-head charges, antlers clashing. These battles look and sound alarming, but fighting males rarely kill each other – the contest is over when the winner has chased off the loser. A fight to the death would not be in the interests of the species' survival.

white eye stripe. Other species, except for the Egyptian plover, are similar. The Egyptian plover, a courser despite its name, is a beautiful gray and white, with black and green markings. Coursers are good runners. They live in the *Old World*, from Africa to Australia.

ORDER: Charadriiformes
FAMILY: Glareolidae

Cowbird

Most species of cowbirds have the habit of laying their eggs in the nests of other birds. In this respect they are like CUCKOOS. Cowbirds are small birds with glossy, dark plumage. Most live in South America. The brown-headed cowbird is a North American species found right across the United States. Cowbirds eat seeds and insects and their name originates from their habit of following cattle and other large animals to feed on insects disturbed by the animal's hooves.

ORDER: Passeriformes
FAMILY: Icteridae

Cowrie

A group of sea snails with colorful, egg-shaped shells. The opening in the underside of the cowrie shell is in the form of a narrow slit. The largest of the 150 species live in warm, tropical waters, but a few species are found around European shores. A live cowrie hides most of its shell by folding part of

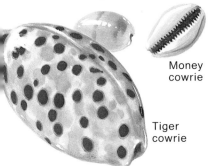

Cowrie shells are popular with collectors. One species was once used as money.

Money cowrie

Tiger cowrie

The **coyote** is found from Alaska to Central America.

the *mantle*, a soft layer of tissue on which the shell forms, over the top of the shell. Cowries crawl over the shallow seabed, feeding on other sea creatures. The more colorful and shiny shells are popular with collectors. People in parts of Africa and southern Asia once used shells of one species as money, while chiefs in Tonga and Fiji wore golden cowrie shells as badges of rank.

CLASS: Gastropoda
ORDER: Mesogastropoda
FAMILY: Cypraeidae

Coyote

The coyote, also called a prairie wolf, is like a small version of the wolf. It measures about 4 ft. (1.2 m) from its nose to the tip of its tail and weighs 20 to 50 lb. (9 to 23 kg). The fur is tawny and the tail, which is bushy with a black tip, droops low behind the hind legs.

Originally coyotes inhabited the plains of western North America. Today, they are even known to enter towns to scavenge among garbage. Despite persecution, they have extended their range and are now found all over North America, even as far north as Alaska.

Coyotes eat a wide range of food – small mammals, birds, fish, insects, and sometimes vegetable matter. They pair for life. Mating occurs between January and March. The cubs (up to 19 in a litter) are born 63 days later and are reared for the first month in a den. This is usually an abandoned burrow, enlarged to form a long tunnel and a nesting chamber.

ORDER: Carnivora
FAMILY: Canidae
SPECIES: *Canis latrans*

Coypu

The coypu is an aquatic RODENT found in South America. Although related to the PORCUPINE, the coypu looks more like a giant rat. It is over 1 yd. (1 m) long, has webbed hind feet and is an excellent swimmer. Its fur is known as nutria.

Coypus live solitary lives in rivers and swamps, feeding on reeds, water grasses, and the roots of water plants. They also eat snails and mussels and will raid farm crops at night. In the 1930s coypus were brought to Europe and reared in captivity for their fur. Some animals escaped and there are now wild coypu colonies in many parts of Europe as well as in North America and Russia. With no natural enemies to control their numbers, these immigrant coypu have become pests. In their native home, the animals are preyed upon by jaguars and caimans.

ORDER: Rodentia
FAMILY: Capromyidae
SPECIES: *Myocastor coypus*

Coypus have become pests in some areas where they were once reared for their fur.

Crab

Crab is the name given to about 4,500 species of CRUSTACEANS. They range in size from the tiny pea crabs, which have shells only .2 in. (6 mm) across, to the giant spider crab of Japan which has a shell of 12 in. (30 cm) across and a claw span of up to 12 ft. (3.7 m). Most species of crabs have hard shells. The hermit crab is an exception in that it does not have a shell covering the whole of its body, but makes its home in the shell of a sea snail or other MOLLUSK. The true crabs have five pairs of legs, though in some species not all the legs are visible. The front pair have well-developed pincers, which are used for picking up food, and many species use the back pair of legs as paddles for swimming. The tail is usually very small and folded forward under the rest of the body. On land, crabs walk with a side-long gait.

Most crabs live in the sea and those which live some distance

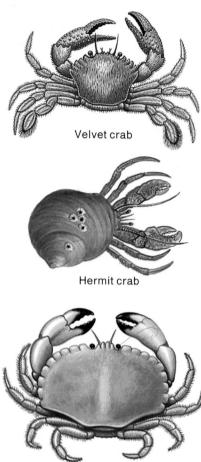

Velvet crab

Hermit crab

Edible crab

A **crab** shows its well-developed pincer legs.

from it return to the water to breed. Some spend all their lives in fresh water; others, such as the Chinese mitten crab, spend most of their time in fresh water, but return to the sea to breed.

Crabs vary considerably in what they eat. Some are vegetarian, some are carnivores, while other crabs eat anything and act as scavengers.

ORDER: Decapoda

Crab spider

These spiders get their name because they resemble crabs in the shape of their legs and the way they scuttle sideways. Crab spiders eat a wide variety of animals. They do not make a web, but lie in wait for their prey among leaf litter or flowers which they often match perfectly. Indeed, the "white death" spider can change its color from white to yellow and vice versa to match different flowers. If it is moved from its white or yellow surroundings to a flower of a different hue it quickly looks for a flower of its own color. The male of one species binds the legs of the

A **crab spider**, camouflaged against the flower on which it lies, has captured a fly.

female to the ground with silk so that he does not get eaten by her after mating – a fate which often overtakes other male crab spiders.

ORDER: Araneae
FAMILIES: Sparassidae, Thomisidae

Crane
N, R, V, E

Cranes are long-necked and long-legged birds of marshlands and swamps. The largest crane stands

One of the most handsome of **cranes**, the crowned crane of southern Africa.

5 ft. (150 cm) high with a wing-span of 7.5 ft. (2.3 m). Cranes live in North America and throughout most of Europe, Asia, and Africa. They are mainly vegetarian, but may also eat frogs and other small animals.

Cranes are well known for their spectacular dances, which are held throughout the year but are most often seen during the breeding season. The birds, in pairs or flocks, walk around each other with quick, stiff-legged steps and wings half spread, sometimes bowing and stretching. The tempo of the dance quickens and the birds leap 14.5 ft. (4.5 m) or more into the air and drift down in a slow-motion ballet. They also pick up sticks or leaves with their bills, throw them into the air and stab at them as they fall. Hunting and the drainage of marshes have caused the numbers of cranes to decline. The whooping crane of North America has declined to a single flock that has been down to 22 birds. A single disaster could wipe them out, particularly during migration, when the birds cannot be protected.

ORDER: Gruiformes
FAMILY: Gruidae

Crane fly

The crane flies are slim-bodied flies with long, slender legs, from

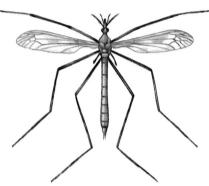

The female **crane fly** is one of the species known as daddy-longlegs.

which they get their popular name of daddy-longlegs. The legs break off very easily, but the insects are not inconvenienced as long as they keep three or four. The narrow wings span 2 in. (5 cm) or more in the larger species, and are often held well away from the body at rest. The *larvae* of many species live in mud and water, but some live in the soil and are troublesome pests because they damage plant roots. They are called leather-jackets. Adult crane flies, which are most abundant in late summer, rarely feed.

ORDER: Diptera
FAMILY: Tipulidae

The **crayfish** usually hides by day under stones or in holes in the bank and hunts by night.

Crayfish
N, R, V, E

Crayfish are freshwater CRUSTA-CEANS which look like small LOBSTERS. They are found in lakes and rivers of all the continents except Africa. They range in size from 1 to 16 in. (2.5 cm to 40 cm).

The head and *thorax* of the crayfish are covered with a single shell. The crayfish has a pair of strong jaws and two pairs of smaller jaws, called *maxillae*. The thorax carries three pairs of

appendages which are used to pass food to its jaws, a pair of stout pincers used to capture and hold the prey, and four pairs of legs used for walking. Other limbs called *swimmerets*, used for swimming, are on the abdomen. The crayfish can swim swiftly backward to escape an enemy.

ORDER: Decapoda
FAMILIES: Parastacidae, Astacidae, Austroastacidae

Cricket

There are about 2,500 species of cricket, most of which live in tropical regions. They are mainly nocturnal, but the European field cricket sings in the fields by day. The house cricket is found all over the world, but it is a native of the Middle East.

True crickets differ from BUSH CRICKETS and GRASSHOPPERS in being flatter and broader across the back. Their jumping legs are also less obvious than in the other groups. The female has a long, needlelike *ovipositor*, with which she usually lays her eggs in the soil, and both sexes have two fairly long tails. Like the bush crickets,

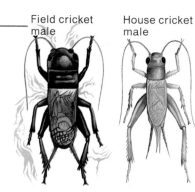

Field cricket male

House cricket male

Crickets can easily be distinguished from grasshoppers by their long, thin antennae.

the males sing, by rubbing their wing bases together, and their calls are often very shrill. Crickets are OMNIVOROUS and most live on the ground. Some can fly, but many have no hind wings and some have no wings at all. Crickets grow up without a pupal stage.

The North American snowy tree cricket is commonly known as the "thermometer cricket." A listener can estimate the temperature in degrees Fahrenheit by counting the number of chirps in 15 seconds and adding 40. In China, cricket fighting has been a popular sport for over a thousand years.

ORDER: Orthoptera
FAMILY: Gryllidae

Croaker

The name of perch-like fish which are famous because they can make sounds – not only croaks but also drumming, purring, creaking, and hissing noises. The 160 or so species of croaker, many of which live off the east coast of the United States, make their noises with their swim bladders, which they vibrate like a drumskin or a guitar string. Croakers may make their noises for the same reasons that birds sing, that is, to advertise their territory, attract a mate, and warn off any rivals. They may even use their sounds like a submarine uses its echo-sounder, to discover the depth at which they are swimming.

ORDER: Perciformes
FAMILY: Sciaenidae

Crocodile   N, V, E

The crocodile family includes the largest of all living REPTILES. The biggest crocodile is the estuarine crocodile, which is said to reach

Two large **crocodiles** bask in the sun on a river bank. They are using the sun to regulate their body temperature.

33 ft. (10m) in length. The smallest is the Congo dwarf crocodile, which is fully grown at about 1 yd. (1 m).

Crocodiles are armored, aquatic reptiles related to the ALLIGATOR to which they are similar. Crocodiles live in tropical parts of Africa, Asia, Australia, and the United States. With their bulky bodies and short legs, adults are usually sluggish, although young crocodiles can gallop with the body high up off the ground. Unlike alligators, they are often found in brackish water and sometimes swim out to sea.

Although cold-blooded, crocodiles prevent their body temperature from varying too much by coming ashore at sunrise to bask and then cooling off in the water, as the sun becomes hotter. They float very low, with little more than eyes and nostrils showing.

An adult crocodile catches and eats fish and also traps larger mammals and birds. It captures its prey by lying in wait near game trails or water holes, seizing an antelope or zebra in its jaws and dragging it under water or knocking it over with a blow from its head or tail. Drowning soon stills the victim's struggles. If its prey is large, the crocodile grips the body in its jaws and rolls over and over, tearing off large chunks of flesh.

The Nile crocodile breeds when 5 to 10 years old. Males fight for territories before mating. Each female lays up to 90 eggs in a specially dug pit. When, after four months, the eggs hatch, the mother takes the hatchlings in her mouth down to the water.

ORDER: Crocodilia
FAMILY: Crocodylidae

Crossbill

Crossbills belong to the FINCH family. They have characteristic bills in which the upper and lower parts cross each other. The common or red crossbill breeds all over the world. Crossbills breed only where there are coniferous trees, for they depend on pine, spruce, and larch cones for food, feeding on the seeds which they gouge out with their bills. The female usually lays 4 eggs in an untidy, mossy nest. The chicks are born with ordinary bills: it is only after they leave the nest that the two halves cross over by growing crooked.

ORDER: Passeriformes
FAMILY: Fringillidae
SPECIES: *Loxia curvirostris* (common crossbill)

Crow   N, R, E

The family includes about 100 species. Hooded and carrion crows inhabit large areas of Europe and Asia, the common crow and fish crow live in North America, the collared crow in China, and the pied crow in Africa. The carrion crow and hooded crow interbreed and are regarded as the same species by some. Carrion crows spend most of their time on the ground feeding or perched in trees. They are often confused with ROOKS but lack the gray skin at the base of the beak. They are black all over, though in strong sunlight the plumage is shot with purple and blue. Crows have a long, slow deliberate flight. Their food is very varied, including both plants and animals. The nest is usually in the stout fork of a tree. A female carrion crow lays 4 to 5 eggs at a time and incubates them.

ORDER: Passeriformes
FAMILY: Corvidae

Crowned eagle

This handsome bird of prey gets its name from the crest of black and white feathers on top of its head. It is the most powerful of the African eagles, although smaller than the MARTIAL EAGLE. Up to 30 in. (76 cm) long, the crowned eagle has the broad, rounded wings and long tail of the typical forest eagle. It is seldom seen, for it flies just above or within the forest canopy when hunting, and its nest is hidden in the treetops. Only the scattered bones of its prey beneath the nest site reveal the eagle's presence. Crowned eagles mostly prey on mammals, especially small antelopes and monkeys.

ORDER: Falconiformes
FAMILY: Accipitridae
SPECIES: *Spizaetus coronatus*

The crossed bill of these birds is not always easy to see.

Crows are among the most clever of all birds. They may store food for the winter and open snails by dropping them on a stone.

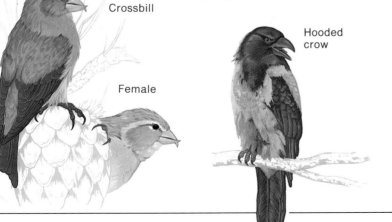

Male Crossbill

Female

Hooded crow

Carrion crow

Crustaceans

The Class Crustacea consists almost entirely of aquatic animals – SHRIMP, CRABS, LOBSTERS, and a host of smaller creatures, such as WATER FLEAS. Many are PLANKTON creatures, drifting in the surface waters of the oceans. The only real land animals in the class are the

The strange face of a **horned-eye crab**.

WOOD LICE, but even these cannot survive in really dry places. The crustaceans have many pairs of limbs, and in the most primitive kinds, such as FAIRY SHRIMP, the limbs are all

alike. More advanced crustaceans have several types of limbs – some for walking, some for swimming, and some for catching food. The gills, which take oxygen from the water, are always modified limbs or outgrowths from the bases of the limbs. The *exoskeleton* is often very hard.

Cuckoo   N, R, V, E, Ex

The cuckoo family gets its name from the distinctive two-note call of the male common cuckoo. No other species in the family utters it. The common cuckoo ranges

Left: A common **cuckoo** just about to make its call; only the male makes the "cuckoo" call; the female has a babbling sound. On the right are the two cuckoo forms.

across Europe, Asia, and America, and all its members are birds that lay their eggs in the nests of other birds.

The Old World cuckoo has distinctive black-and-white barring on its underside, which makes it resemble the SPARROW HAWK. This may help the cuckoo to frighten away birds from their nests when it wishes to lay its eggs. Two common kinds of North American birds are the black-billed cuckoo and the yellow-billed cuckoo. They both have white breasts. Cuckoos mainly eat insects, worms, spiders, and centipedes.

Old World cuckoos lay their eggs in the nests of other birds. The foster parents instinctively feed the young cuckoo when it hatches, even though it pushes any other eggs and chicks out of the nest.

ORDER: Cuculiformes
FAMILY: Cuculidae
SPECIES: *Cuculus canorus* (common)

Curassow   N, V, E

Curassows are birds of the forests of Central and South America. There are 13 species, ranging in size from a pheasant to a small TURKEY, to which they are in fact related. Curassows are mostly black or brown in color, and have crests and bony *casques* on their heads. Unlike other gamebirds, they nest in trees and not on the

Old World cuckoo

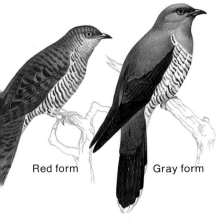

Red form   Gray form

ground. They eat mainly fruit, nuts, buds, and leaves. Curassows would make good domestic birds, for their flesh is tasty. However, they lay few eggs and do not breed well in captivity.

ORDER: Galliformes
FAMILY: Cracidae

On the shore, **curlews** search with their long bills for small crabs, shrimp, and fish.

Curlew

Curlews are large wading birds which are distinguished by their 5-in. (13-cm) down-curved bill, and their two-syllable fluting call from which they get their name. The common curlew is found across Europe and Asia, usually on open plains, moors, and marshes. Curlews feed on shellfish, snails, worms, insects, and fish, using their long bills to probe for them in the sand.

ORDER: Charadriiformes
FAMILY: Scolopacidae
SPECIES: *Numenius arquata* (common)

Cuscus   N, R, E

The cuscus is a noisy PHALANGER. Over 16 species live in the forests of Australia and Papua New Guinea. They are just over 1 yd. (1 m) long, including the curling *prehensile* tail, which is used when climbing. They are nocturnal animals which eat leaves, insects, eggs, and small birds. When

alarmed they may snarl and bark with a guttural sound. They probably have no particular breeding season as most females carry one or more young at any time of the year. The cuscus can produce a repulsive odor that may be defensive.

ORDER: Marsupialia
FAMILY: Phalangeridae

Cuttlefish

The cuttlefish is a MOLLUSK related to the SQUID and the OCTOPUS. It has a shield-shaped body, inside which is a chalky plate containing gas-filled cells which make the animal buoyant. It has a small head bearing eight arms and two long tentacles which it can retract into pockets beside each of its large eyes. The smallest known cuttlefish is 1.6 in. (4 cm) long, the largest 5 ft. (1.5 m). There are about 100 species.

The cuttlefish swims by waving fins on either side of its body, but when speed is required it can eject a stream of water from the funnel, producing a form of jet propulsion. It can also eject a blue-black "ink" which serves as a decoy when danger threatens. Cuttlefish are capable of changing their color. A cuttlefish can change from gray to reddish-brown to a pale green as it passes over various patches of color.

CLASS: Cephalopoda
ORDER: Decapoda

The **cuttlefish** catches its prey by shooting out its long tentacles at lightning speed.

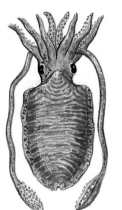

Cuttlebone

D

Dab

The dab is a flatfish, a relative of the FLOUNDER. Like other flatfish of the sea, the dab lies on its side on the seabed, has a twisted mouth, and an eye that has migrated around the head so that both eyes lie on the same side. These peculiar developments happen as the dab grows up: its tiny young, or *fry*, have a more normal fishlike appearance.

The dab reaches a maximum length of about 16 in. (40 cm). The upper surface of its body is brown, with red spots smaller than those of a flounder. The underside of the body is white.

ORDER: Pleuronectiformes
FAMILY: Pleuronectidae
SPECIES: *Limanda limanda*

The **dab** is a common flatfish of sandy or shell grounds.

Damselfish

The damselfish, or demoiselle, is a brilliantly colored and patterned fish that lives on, or near, coral reefs. Damselfish are usually not more than 6 in. (15 cm) long, but they are aggressive and attack and eat other small fish.

The most famous damselfish is the clownfish, which shelters among the stinging tentacles of a giant sea anemone. The clownfish is not stung to death because a special slime on its scales stops the action of the deadly stinging cells. Other fish, however, do get caught and killed by the sea anemone, and then the clownfish probably shares in the anemone's meal.

ORDER: Perciformes
FAMILY: Pomacentridae

Darwin's finches

A group of FINCHES which live only on the Galapagos Islands – except for one species which is also found on Cocos Island. They are named after the naturalist Charles Darwin, who visited the islands during his famous voyage on HMS Beagle in 1835. Isolated on the islands for some time, the finches have evolved into several distinct forms, so taking advantage of the different ways of life open to such birds on the islands. Darwin's observations on these birds were an important influence in helping him draw up his theory of evolution.

These finches are presumed to

Damselfish are small, brightly colored and aggressive.

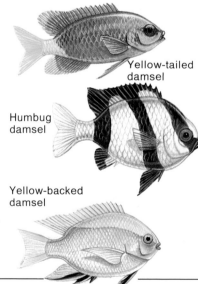

Yellow-tailed damsel

Humbug damsel

Yellow-backed damsel

have developed from ancestors on the South American mainland 600 mi. (960 km) to the east. There are 14 species, each a drab grayish brown. There is little variation except in the bills. This is unusual as the mainland finches differ in plumage rather than body form. The bills are adapted for eating different kinds of food. Some Darwin's finches, such as the ground finches, have stout bills which they use for cracking seeds. Another group, the tree finches, have pointed bills and behave like tits. The remarkable woodpecker-finch climbs up and down trees, digging holes in search of food, which is extracted with the aid of twigs held in the bill.

ORDER: Passeriformes
FAMILY: Fringillidae

Dasyure

Dasyures are known as the native cats of Australia, Tasmania, and New Guinea. They are not in fact true cats but carnivorous MARSUPIALS, related to the marsupial mice. They have short legs and long, bushy tails, and their coats are marked with white spots. The head of some species is weasellike with a pointed muzzle and long whiskers. Three of the five species of dasyure live mainly in trees, exceptions being the quoll and the western native cat. The tree-dwellers have roughened pads that give a good grip while climbing. Dasyures feed on birds, lizards, insects, and young rabbits. They produce up to eight young, though some quoll females have been recorded as having as many as 24.

ORDER: Marsupialia
FAMILY: Dasyuridae

GLOSSARY

Note: Words in bold type indicate a separate glossary entry.

Abdomen The hind part of an animal's body, generally between the **thorax** and pelvis in vertebrates, containing the stomach, intestines, and other organs. In mammals it is separated from the thorax by the diaphragm. In arthropods it is the section behind the thorax.

Albino An animal that lacks coloring or pigment. It often has pale or white skin, hair, or fur, and pink eyes. Albinism is caused by a factor passed down in the animal's genes.

Anal fin In fish, the fin that lies along the underside of the body just behind the anus. The anal fin works with the fish's other fins in swimming, turning, and balancing. (Also see **Dorsal fin**; **Pectoral fin**; **Pelvic fin**)

Antenna Either of a pair of long, thin movable sense organs on the head of an insect or crustacean. Antennae are sometimes called "feelers," and are used for locating and identifying the animal's surroundings.

Barbel A threadlike organ of touch that grows from the lips or jaws of some fish. In general, barbels serve the same purpose as **antennae**.

Binocular vision A kind of vision in which both eyes are used at the same time and move in the same direction.

Bivalve A mollusk, such as an oyster, cockle, mussel, or clam, that has two hinged *valves*, or shells, each usually the mirror image of the other. When the valves are shut the body of the animal is completely enclosed. Under water, a bivalve opens its valves to feed. When it is stranded above the water line at low tide the valves close to prevent the animal's body from drying out.

Canine teeth The pair of teeth in the upper and lower jaw, behind the **incisors**. Canine teeth are generally long and pointed and are used for seizing hold of and piercing the prey.

Carapace Any skeletal shield on an animal's back. It can be the hard **chitinous** covering of some insects or crustaceans, the heavy structures of armadillos, or the bony structures of turtles and tortoises. These are covered with a hornlike material which gives the "shell" its pattern and color.

Cartilage Sometimes called "gristle," cartilage forms the skeleton of the embryos of **vertebrates** and of the adults of a few groups such as sharks and rays. Cartilage, which is firm but flexible, also covers the joints between limb bones in most adult vertebrates and forms the disks between vertebrae in the spine.

Casque A bony shield on the upper surface of the head. In birds it may form the base of the bill, and give the appearance of a helmet on some species.

Cephalopod A member of one of the three largest classes of mollusk. Squids, octopuses, and cuttlefish are all cephalopods, a word meaning "head-foot." Most cephalopods have a head with a sharp, horny beak and muscular tentacles around the mouth. Cephalopods are the only invertebrates to have an eye like that of vertebrates.

Chinin A tough, fibrous material present in **cuticle** which forms the **exoskeleton** of insects and crustaceans. It performs a similar role to bone in vertebrates, making the body rigid and protecting the internal organs.

Chordate A member of the phylum Chordata, which includes all the vertebrates. All chordates at some stage of their development have gill slits, a **notochord**, and a spinal nerve cord.

Chrysalis In the life cycle of butterflies and moths, the stage that occurs between the last larval stage and the adult. In the chrysalis stage the insect goes through a complicated **metamorphosis** before emerging as an adult. The term **pupa** is used to refer to the similar stage in flies, ants, bees, wasps, and beetles.

Cilia Hairlike projections that cover the surfaces of certain animal cells. Their main function is to move fluids over the cell surface, which they do by moving together with a rhythmical beating motion in a constant direction. Single-cell animals, called protozoa, use cilia for swimming. Epithelial cells which line the nose and windpipe use cilia to move fluid (mucus) that carries dust and germs away from the lungs.

Cocoon A silky or fibrous case which the larvae of certain insects spin around themselves to shelter them during the **pupa** stage. The cocoons of spiders, earthworms, and leeches are produced to protect their eggs.

Cornicle A small, hornlike projection, as in the horns, or tentacles, on the head of a snail. Cornicles are used as sensory organs. Many land snails have two pairs of cornicles, with their eyes at the tips of the top pair.

Crinoid A word meaning "lily-shaped," used to refer to members of the class Crinoidea of sea animals, such as the sea lily and feather star, which resemble flowers.

Cuticle The tough outer covering of the bodies of many invertebrates such as insects and crustaceans. It is secreted by the epidermis underneath and may be coated with wax to prevent water loss.

Dorsal fin In fish, the fin that lies along the spine on the upper side of the body. The dorsal fin works with the fish's other fins in swimming, turning, and balancing. (See **Anal fin**; **Pectoral fin**; **Pelvic fin**)

Elytra The front pair of tough, thickened wings in beetles which act as a protective covering for the more delicate rear wings.

Exoskeleton The hard supporting structure on the outside of the body of an invertebrate. Its function is similar to that of the bone or cartilage endoskeleton found inside a vertebrate. The material from which the exoskeleton is formed is secreted from the animal's body.

Flagella The tiny, whiplike parts of

some bacteria and protozoans that are used to propel these organisms through their fluid surroundings. The word is also used to describe the thin, lashlike tips of the antennae in many insects.

Frenulum A tiny, stiff, bristlelike structure on the hind wing of some moths that locks into hooks on the front wing to link the wings together during flight.

Fry Newly-hatched young fish. Fry also sometimes refers to small adult fish, expecially when they are in large groups.

Gall A thick swelling or tumor, produced by a plant in response to the presence of an insect or other creature on its tissues. The plant is not seriously harmed and the invading animal lives and feeds quite happily in the swelling until fully grown. Gall wasps are the best known of the gall causers.

Gestation period The period from conception to birth in mammals, which varies from a few weeks in animals such as mice, to 22 months in the elephant, the longest gestation period of any animal.

Gizzard A part of the digestive tract, especially in birds, that is specialized for breaking down food. The walls of the gizzard are thick and muscular and the food is ground up for digestion by small stones and grit swallowed by the bird.

Grub The short, fat **larva** of some insects, especially beetles.

Herbivore The opposite of a carnivore – that is, any animal that eats only plant material rather than flesh. Grazing animals such as horses, sheep, and cattle are all herbivores. Animals that eat both plants and meat are called omnivores.

Hermaphrodite An animal with the sexual organs of both male and female. Some hermaphrodites, such as certain earthworms, can function as male and female at the same time, though they must mate with another individual. Others, such as prawns and limpets, are male at a certain stage in their lives and female at another. (Also see **Intersexes**)

Hormone A chemical messenger produced in one part of the body, such as in the thyroid, adrenal, and pituitary glands, which is transported to another part to stimulate activity, growth, or reproduction or to regulate metabolism.

Hybrid An animal or plant that is the result of a cross-breeding between two distinct species. A mule, for example, is the result of a cross between a donkey (jackass) and a horse (mare). A mule, like most other animal hybrids, is sterile – that is, it cannot reproduce.

Incisor Any of the wide, chisellike teeth between the **canines** in carnivores that are used for cutting rather than tearing or grinding. Herbivores, such as rodents, have especially large incisors for gnawing. Because they wear down quickly, rodents' incisors grow continuously from the roots.

Intersexes Certain species of animal that undergo sex reversal to change from male to female or vice versa. The sex of some frogs and crustaceans can be altered by changing the temperature of their surroundings. The European flat oyster can reverse its sex several times.

Invertebrate Any of the large group of animals without backbones. Of the million or more species of animal only about 42,000 are **vertebrates** (backboned animals) – the rest are invertebrates. Sponges, jellyfish, worms, insects, crustaceans, and mollusks are all invertebrates.

Keratin A tough, fibrous protein that forms the major part of hair, nails, claws, and horn in animals.

Larva A preadult stage in the development of many animals, especially insects. The larvae of animals look completely different from the adult and may go through several stages before reaching adulthood. For example, caterpillars are the larvae of moths and butterflies, maggots are the larvae of flies, and grubs are the larvae of certain beetles. In the same way a tadpole is the larval stage of a frog. Unlike the adults, the larval stages of the frog, mosquito and caddis fly live entirely in the water. Insect larvae go through a

complete **metamorphosis** to become an adult. (See **pupa**)

Mandible The lower jaw of vertebrates, or one of a pair of arthropod mouthparts.

Mantle The soft flap or folds of the body wall of a mollusk such as a mussel or clam. The mantle usually secretes the fluid from which the shell is formed.

Metabolism The process by which food is built up into living material or used to supply energy in a living organism.

Metamorphosis A word meaning "transformation," used to refer to the change in form and structure during the development of some animals from the larval to the adult stage. In many insects metamorphosis takes place in the pupa or chrysalis, when the wormlike larva is transformed into an adult, winged insect. (See **Chrysalis**; **Larva**; **Pupa**)

Molar Any of the large, flat cheek teeth in mammals that are used for grinding and chewing food. Large herbivores, such as horses and cows, have very high, wide molars that can take a lot of wear before they are ground down. An elephant deals with wear in a different way. Each of its teeth is so long, wide, and deep that it takes up one whole side of its jaw. As each tooth wears down it is shed and a new one moves down from the gums to replace it.

Molt To shed the skin, fur, feathers, or other outer covering of the body. Animals such as snakes, insects, and crustaceans shed their skin, or **cuticle**, as they grow in order to accommodate their larger body. Molting in birds and mammals is often a seasonal occurrence which prepares them for the heat in summer. It also applies to young animals as they develop their adult plumage or coat.

Musk A substance with a strong, penetrating odor secreted from a gland by certain animals such as the male musk deer, muskrat, badger, and others. The odor is usually released during the breeding season. Musk is used as a basis for many perfumes.

Mutant An animal that does not conform in appearance or structure to the rest of its species because of a change, or mutation, in its genes. Most mutations, such as extra horns or toes or different coloring, are disadvantageous to an animal. These mutations are eventually extinguished through natural selection. But some mutant genes become dominant when, for example, the animal's environment changes. One dramatic example of this is the peppered moth. Normally it is mottled gray to blend in with the lichens on the bark of trees where it rests. Occasionally a mutation takes place that produces a black moth which, easily seen by predators on the gray lichen, has little chance of surviving. But in industrial areas where pollution has killed the lichens on the trees and turned them black, the black mutant moth survives successfully.

New World A term used to describe animals that come from the Western Hemisphere. Animals native to the Eastern Hemisphere are described as **Old World**. For example, the New World monkeys of Central and South America have evolved to become noticeably different from their Old World relatives in Europe, Africa, and Asia.

Notochord A primitive form of backbone present at some stage in the development of all **chordates**. In adult vertebrates it is replaced by the cartilage, or bone, that forms the spinal column. The function of the notochord is roughly the same as that of the spine – that is, to support the body and keep it rigid.

Nymph A stage in the development of certain insects such as grasshoppers and dragonflies. A nymph resembles the adult but is usually wingless. A dragonfly nymph with wing buds spends its early life in the water and then climbs up a plant stem into the air It then sheds its skin and the fully adult dragonfly emerges.

Old World A term used to refer to animal species native to Europe, Asia, or Africa to distinguish them from similar species of the **New World** – that is, North, Central, and South America.

Operculum Any of a number of flaps or lidlike structures in plants or animals, such as the hard, bony covering that protects the gills of fish, or the chalky plates that form the "lid" at the top of an acorn barnacle.

Opposable Capable of being applied so as to meet another part. In zoology the term is most often used to refer to the opposable thumb (and big toe) of primates which are capable of grasping and other complex movements.

Ovipositor A long, thin hollow organ found at the end of the abdomen of some female insects used for depositing eggs in a suitable place, such as inside plant or animal tissue.

Ovum A Latin word meaning "egg," used to refer to the mature female germ cell of an animal which, if fertilized, develops into a new individual of the same species.

Parapodia Tiny limblike projections found on the bodies of segmented worms, such as bristleworms, used for locomotion.

Parthenogenesis Reproduction through the development of an unfertilized ovum as in certain polyzoans and insects. Artificial parthenogenesis is the development of an ovum stimulated by chemical or mechanical means.

Pectoral fin In fish, either of a pair of fins that lie on either side of the body just behind the head. The pectoral fins correspond to the forelimbs of a higher vertebrate and work with the fish's other fins in swimming, turning, and balancing. (See **Anal fin; Dorsal fin; Pelvic fin**)

Pelvic fin In fish, either of a pair of fins that lie on either side of the body in the pelvic region. The pelvic fins correspond to the hind limbs of higher vertebrates. (See **Anal fin; Dorsal fin; Pectoral fin**)

Photosynthesis The process by which green plants "manufacture" food from carbon dioxide and water in the presence of light, with the help of the chlorophyll found in their leaves.

Pigments Any coloring matter in the cells and tissues of plants or animals. One common animal pigment is melanin. This is a dark pigment that is present to a greater degree in, for example, the skin and hair of Afro-Americans, and to a lesser degree, in a Caucasian. Most mammals have hair pigmented by melanin. Even hemoglobin in the blood of vertebrates is a pigment, giving the blood its red color. Another red pigment is cochineal, extracted from a scale insect and used for making dyes.

Placenta The structure that develops inside the uterus of a mammal during **gestation**. It is anchored to the wall of the uterus and is connected to the developing embryo by the **umbilical cord**. It is through the placenta that oxygen and nourishment are passed from the mother to the fetus. Wastes from the fetus pass through the placenta and into the mother's bloodstream. The placenta is discharged from the body shortly after birth.

Polyp Any of a group of sea animals in the phylum Coelenterata, such as the sea anemone and the hydra. They have a mouth fringed with many small tentacles bearing stinging cells, at the top of a tubelike body.

Preen gland An oil gland found on the outside of a bird's body near the base of the tail. The gland secretes an oily substance which is squeezed out by the bird's bill as it preens, or cleans itself, and is distributed over the feathers. Water birds, such as ducks, have well-developed preen glands and it is thought that oiling their feathers helps to waterproof them. Not all birds have preen glands.

Prehensile Adapted for seizing or grasping, as the tail of a monkey or the trunk of an elephant.

Primates The order of mammals that includes humans, apes, monkeys, bushbabies, pottos, lemurs, and the tarsier. Primates have hands and feet with fingers and toes adapted for grasping, comparatively larger brains than other mammals, and nails instead of claws.

Proboscis A tubular organ used for sucking, food gathering, or sensing.

Both the elephant's trunk and the tapir's long, flexible snout are kinds of proboscis, as are the organs with similar functions of some insects, worms, and mollusks.

Prolegs The short, fleshy limbs attached to the abdomens of certain insect larvae such as caterpillars. They are used for locomotion.

Protein Any of a large group of substances made up of a complex union of amino acids that occur in all animal and plant matter. Proteins are the most important chemical components of all living matter. They play an essential part in the structure and functioning of animals: enzymes, hemoglobin, many hormones, and antibodies are just some of the many different kinds of proteins necessary for life.

Pupa A stage in the development of many insects in which the wormlike **larva** is transformed into the adult form. When it enters the pupal stage, the larva ceases feeding and moving and often hides itself inside a **cocoon**. The pupa ''rests'' while complete **metamorphosis** takes place, and emerges from the cocoon, or pupal case, as an adult. The pupa of a butterfly is called a **chrysalis**.

Radula Found in most mollusks, a ribbonlike structure with rows of small teeth, or scrapers, that tear up food and take it into the mouth.

Respiration In animals, the process of taking in oxygen and releasing carbon dioxide, whether through the skin, or by means of lungs or gills. Respiration continues inside the body as each individual cell is fed with oxygen carried in the bloodstream from the lungs or gills as part of the energy-producing process.

Savanna A grassland, often with just a few, scattered trees, especially in tropical or subtropical areas that have seasonal rains. The savanna is a habitat for certain species of animal specially adapted to survive there.

Siphon A tubular organ in some animals used for the intake and output of water. Some burrowing **bivalve** mollusks use their siphons to draw in fresh sea water bearing food and oxygen. Cuttlefish use their siphons, or funnels, like jets for locomotion. Water is ejected from the siphon with great force, so the animals are propelled along.

Snow line The boundary in altitude above which the temperature is so low all year-round that the snow never melts, as on the tops of high mountains.

Spinneret the organ in spiders and caterpillars with which they spin silky threads for webs or cocoons.

Swim bladder A gas-filled sac inside the body cavity of most bony fish which gives them buoyancy in the water. Some fish also use them for breathing. Sharks do not have a swim bladder.

Swimmeret Any of the small appendages on the abdomen of some crustaceans, such as lobsters and crayfish, used for swimming and for carrying eggs.

Thorax In insects, the middle segment of the three main segments – head, thorax, **abdomen** – of the body. In higher vertebrates, the thorax is the chest, the part of the body between the neck and the abdomen, containing the heart and the lungs.

Tree line The line above or beyond which trees do not grow, as on high mountains or in polar regions.

Tundra The vast, treeless plains of Arctic regions. Most of the tundra is in the Arctic Circle. In winter the tundra is snow-covered. Even in summer the temperature is near freezing and only tough mosses, lichens, and dwarfed plants grow. These support animals adapted to the harsh climate.

Umbilical cord A tough, cablelike structure that connects a fetus (at the navel) with the **placenta**. All nutrients and oxygen pass through the umbilical cord to the growing fetus, as does waste from the fetus to the mother's bloodstream. At birth, when the newborn's own circulatory and respiratory systems take over, the umbilical cord is severed. Any remaining portion soon dries up and falls off.

Ungulate A term that means "having hoofs," used to describe the group of hoofed mammals that includes cows, horses, deer, goats, pigs, camels, etc.

Valve The shell of a mollusk. In **bivalve** mollusks the shell has two parts, such as that of a mussel or clam. The word valve is also used in anatomy to describe a membraneous fold or structure that permits body fluids to flow in one direction only, such as in the heart or blood vessels. A valve may also open or close a tube or opening.

Vertebrate Any of the group of **chordate** animals with segmented backbones – the opposite of an **invertebrate**. All mammals, fish, birds, repitiles, and amphibians are vertebrates.

Wattle A fleshy, wrinkled piece of skin that hangs from the chin or throat of certain birds, such as the turkey or cockerel, or from some lizards.

ALTERNATIVE NAMES
AND ADDITIONAL CROSS-REFERENCES

A
African Wild Dog *see* Cape Hunting Dog
Andean Bear *see* Spectacled Bear
Apara *see* Armadillo
Armored Sea Robbin *see* Gurnard
Army Worm *see* Noctuid Moth
Arum Frog *see* Reed Frog

B
Bamboo Rat *see* Mole Rat
Banded Anteater *see* Numbat
Barbary Stag *see* Red Deer
Barking Deer *see* Muntjac
Bearded Vulture *see* Lammergeier
Bell Toad *see* Midwife Toad
Bengalese Finch *see* Mannikin
Bezoar *see* Ibex
Bilby *see* Bandicoot
Blackfly *see* Aphid
Black Panther *see* Leopard
Bloody-nosed Beetle *see* Leaf Beetle
Blue-bottle *see* Blowfly
Blue Monkey *see* Guenon
Bobak *see* Marmot
Book Scorpion *see* False Scorpion
Brown Creeper *see* Tree Creeper
Burbot *see* Ling
Butcherbird *see* Shrike

C
Cabezon *see* Sculpin
Cake Urchin *see* Sand Dollar
Camberwell Beauty *see* Vanessid Butterfly
Camel Spider *see* Solifugid
Carpet Shark *see* Wobbegong
Cat Bear *see* Red Panda
Cavie *see* Guinea Pig
Chickadee *see* Tit
Chital *see* Axis Deer
Clownfish *see* Damsel Fish
Cockatiel *see* Cockatoo
Colies *see* Mousebird
Comma *see* Vanessid Butterfly
Crab-eating Monkey *see* Macaque
Crawfish *see* Spiny Lobster
Cross Spider *see* Orb Spider
Cutworm *see* Noctuid Moth

D
Dabchick *see* Grebe
Damsel Fly *see* Dragonfly
Demoiselle *see* Damselfish
Desert Rat *see* Jerboa
Diadem Spider *see* Orb Spider

Drill *see* Mandrill
Driver Ant *see* Army Ant
Drone Fly *see* Hoverfly
Dublin Prawn *see* Lobster
Duckbill *see* Platypus
Dugong *see* Sea Cow
Dunnock *see* Accentor
Dust Lice *see* Book Lice
Dwarf Buffalo *see* Anoa

E
Eared Seal *see* Fur Seal
Eared Seal *see* Sea Lion
Earthcreeper *see* Ovenbird
Echidna *see* Spiny Anteater
Edible Snail *see* Roman Snail
Eel-pout *see* Ling
Elk *see* Moose
Elk *see* Red Deer
Euro *see* Kangaroo

F
Feral Pigeon *see* Rock Dove
Ferret *see* Polecat
Finback Whale *see* Rorqual
Firecrest *see* Goldcrest
Fire Fox *see* Red Panda
Fisher *see* Marten
Fish Hawk *see* Osprey
Flea Beetle *see* Leaf Beetle
Flying Gurnard *see* Flyingfish
Fox Cat *see* Red Panda

G
Galago *see* Bushbaby
Galah *see* Cockatoo
Gang-gang *see* Cockatoo
Garfish *see* Needlefish
Gayol *see* Gaur
Gemsbok *see* Oryx
Giraffe-necked Gazelle *see* Gerenuk
Glutton *see* Wolverine
Goosander *see* Merganser
Grampus *see* Killer Whale
Great Auk *see* Little Auk
Great White Heron *see* Egret
Greenbottle *see* Blowfly
Greenfly *see* Aphid
Green Monkey *see* Vervet Monkey
Green Plover *see* Lapwing
Grizzly Bear *see* Brown Bear
Grosbeak *see* Hawfinch
Gymnosome *see* Sea Butterfly

H
Hairy Hedgehog *see* Gymnure
Hamadryas *see* Baboon

Harvest Spider *see* Harvestman
Hedge Sparrow *see* Accentor
Henfish *see* Lampsucker
Himalayan Raccoon *see* Red Panda
Hog Deer *see* Axis Deer
Honey Bear *see* Kinkajou
Hoose Mackerel *see* Scad
Horned Rattlesnake *see* Sidewider
Horntail *see* Sawfly
Horse Mackerel *see* Scad
Horseshoe Crab *see* King Crab
Hydroid *see* Sea Fir

I
Inchworm *see* Geometer Moth
Indian Antelope *see* Blackbuck

J
Jabiru *see* Stork
Jack *see* Scad
Jaeger *see* Skua
Java Sparrow *see* Mannikin
Jewel Thrush *see* Pitta

K
Katydid *see* Bush Cricket
Kodiak Bear *see* Brown Bear
Kokako *see* Wattlebird

L
Lampern *see* Lamprey
Laughing Jackass *see* Kookaburra
Leatherhead *see* Honey Eater
Leatherjacket *see* Crane Fly
Lechwe *see* Antelope
Legionary Ant *see* Army Ant
Lily-trotter *see* Jacana
Loon *see* Diver
Looper *see* Geometer Moth
Lotus Bird *see* Jacana

M
Manatee *see* Sea Cow
Maneater Shark *see* Great White Shark
Man-o'war Bird *see* Frigate Bird
Manta Ray *see* Devilfish
Marbled White Butterfly *see* Brown Butterfly
Marsupial Anteater *see* Numbat
May Bug *see* Cockchafer
Mealy Bug *see* Scale Insect
Meercat *see* Suricate
Milkweed Butterfly *see* Monarch Butterfly
Miner *see* Ovenbird
Mithan *see* Gaur

Moon Rat *see* Gymnure
Mother Carey's Chicken *see* Storm
  Petrel
Mourning Cloak *see* Vanessid
  Butterfly
Mousehare *see* Pika
Murre *see* Guillemot
Mustang *see* Horse
Muttonbird *see* Shearwater

N
Ne-ne *see* Hawaiian Goose
Night Monkey *see* Douroucouli

O
O-o-aa *see* Honey Eater
Otter-cat *see* Jaguarundi
Owl Monkey *see* Douroucouli
Owlet Moth *see* Noctuid Moth

P
Painted Lady *see* Vanessid Butterfly
Panther *see* Leopard
Peacock *see* Peafowl
Peacock Butterfly *see* Vanessid
  Butterfly
Peewit *see* Lapwing
Pigeon *see* Dove
Pigeon *see* Rock Dove
Pigeon Hawk *see* Merlin
Plant Lice *see* Aphid
Pollock *see* Coalfish
Possum *see* Phalanger
Prairie Wolf *see* Coyote
Praying Mantis *see* Mantis
Przewalski's Horse *see* Horse
Puku *see* Kob

Q
Quoll *see* Dasyure

R
Rainbow Fish *see* Guppy
Ratel *see* Honey Badger
Red Admiral *see* Vanessid Butterfly
Red-tailed Monkey *see* Guenon
Ribbonfish *see* Oarfish
Rock-borer *see* Piddock

Rock Coney *see* Pika
Rock Rabbit *see* Pika

S
Saithe *see* Coalfish
Salp *see* Sea Squirt
Sand Rat *see* Gerbil
Sardine *see* Pilchard
Sawbill *see* Merganser
Scaly Anteater *see* Pangolin
Scrub Wallaby *see* Pademelon
Sea Biscuit *see* Sand Dollar
Sexton Beetle *see* Burying Beetle
Shag *see* Cormorant
Shaketail *see* Ovenbird
Short-tailed Weasel *see* Stoat
Siamang *see* Gibbon
Siamese Fighting Fish *see* Fighting
  Fish
Sitatunga *see* Nyah
Snowshoe Rabbit *see* Hare
Soapfish *see* Grouper
Spanish Fly *see* Blister Beetle
Spice Finch *see* Mannikin
Spinebill *see* Honey Eater
Spotted Cavy *see* Paca
Stink Bug *see* Shield Bug
Stout *see* Horsefly
Sunfish *see* Ocean Sunfish
Sunspider *see* Solifugid

T
Tamandua *see* Anteater
Tatler *see* Sandpiper
Terrapin *see* Tortoises and Turtles
Thecosome *see* Sea Butterfly
Thorny Devil *see* Moloch
Thylacine *see* Tasmanian Wolf
Tickbird *see* Oxpecker
Tiddler *see* Stickleback
Tieke *see* Wattlebird
Titmouse *see* Tit
Tizi *see* Bush Cricket
Torpedo *see* Electric Ray
Tortoise Beetle *see* Leaf Beetle
Tortoiseshell Butterfly *see* Vanessid
  Butterfly
Trader Rat *see* Pack Rat

Tree Fox *see* Gray Fox
Tumblebug *see* Scarab Beetle
Tunnel-web Spider *see* Sheet Web
  Spider
Tunny *see* Tuna
Tur *see* Ibex
Turtle *see* Tortoises and Turtles

W
Walking Stick *see* Stick Insect
Wallaroo *see* Kangaroo
Waller's Gazelle *see* Gerenuk
Wapiti *see* Red Deer
Water Boa *see* Anaconda
Water Buffalo *see* Indian Buffalo
Water strider *see* Pond Skater
Wels *see* Catfish
Western Native Cat *see* Dasyure
Wheel Animalcule *see* Rotifer
Whistling Duck *see* Tree Duck
Whistling Hare *see* Pika
White Curlew *see* Ibis
White Death Spider *see* Crab
  Spider
White Whale *see* Beluga
Whooping Crane *see* Crane
Widow-bird *see* Whydah
Wigeon *see* Duck
Wildebeest *see* Gnu
Wind Scorpion *see* Solifugid
Winkle *see* Periwinkle
Wireworm *see* Click Beetle
Wisent *see* Bison
Wood Rat *see* Pack Rat
Wood Wasp *see* Sawfly
Woodworm *see* Furniture Beetle
Worm Lizards *see* Amphisbaena
Wreckfish *see* Bass

Y
Yellowjacket *see* Wasp
Yellowshafted Flicker *see*
  Yellowhammer

Z
Zebra Antelope *see* Duiker

INDEX

Page numbers in *italics* refer
to illustrations.